Making *of a* MARRIAGE

Building Healthy, Whole People and Marriages that Last a Lifetime

BRENT SHARPE MS, LMFT, LPC
JANIS SHARPE MS, LMFT

CONTENTS

Acknowledgments

THERE ARE MANY WHO HAVE encouraged us throughout the years to put our work in writing. We want to say thank you to Dr. Ed and Judy Tarr and Dr. Jerry Duncan for your consistent support, wisdom, and friendship over the past twenty years. Jeff and Lori Voth and The Life Connection church family for partnering with us in ministry. Jake Jones for believing in this project and guiding us; Stuart and Kim Hook and Brad and Jessica Sheasby for your valuable perspectives on the material.

To our parents, Bob and Lois Jean Sharpe and Don and Ruth Roberts, for your commitments to each other and for showing us how to stand the test of time in marriage and flourish in your love for each other.

To our children, Preston, Kaitlin, Spencer, and Hayley who have been so supportive with the "stretch" this project put on all of us as a family and who have shown us the reason for a committed, unified and loving marriage.

And, most importantly, to our guiding force, Jesus Christ, who has shown us what love looks like by loving us in an amazing way and giving us the ability to love each other.

INTRODUCTION

THROUGHOUT NEARLY THIRTY YEARS OF experiencing a growing and thriving marriage ourselves, and twenty-five years of professionally helping other couples find the keys to success in their relationships, we have found that marriage can be exhilarating, confusing, wonderful, disappointing, peaceful, and frustrating—the closest thing to heaven or the closest thing to hell, depending on how the day is going! Why is it that this relationship, that we seem to naturally desire, can start out with such great anticipation, and yet almost one out of two end in utter discouragement and even cease to exist?

Between the two of us, we have worked with literally thousands of couples in either premarital or marriage counseling, in weekend seminars, or as members of our church. Through these experiences, we have seen the wonder of God's plan for marriage shine forth, but at the same time we have realized that there has been a sadistic attack unleashed in the world to destroy this most precious and God-breathed institution.

We have seen common threads throughout relationships—key building blocks to a healthy marriage. Perhaps most obvious, healthy marriages, much like healthy individuals, are products of healthy habits or disciplines. Just as our own personal spiritual life is formed through a lifetime of daily experiences in which we turn our wills over to God, so a God-formed marriage is developed through daily behaviors in which each individual is focused on how his or her outward actions can inspire life in the other.

We recognize that it is only by God's grace that we have found health in our own relationship and discovered the principles that we share in the pages of this book. We entered marriage unadvised, with idealism in our hearts, and found through an uneven journey the need for something outside ourselves to traverse the rapids we experienced. It is through God's grace, desperate hearts, quality professional training, and years of experience hearing thousands of stories that we share the insights in the chapters to come.

Whether you are on a journey to enrich your relationship, learn principles to help you on your way, or have lost hope in the vision you started with, we pray that you will find nuggets of truth imbedded in these pages that will allow you to experience the wonder of God's heart for your marriage.

I pray that out of his glorious riches he may strengthen you with power through his Spirit in your inner being, so that Christ may dwell in your hearts through faith. And I pray that you, being rooted and established in love, may have power, together with all the saints, to grasp how wide and long and high and deep is the love of Christ, and to know this love that surpasses knowledge—that you may be filled to the measure of all the fullness of God. Now to him who is able to do immeasurably more than all we ask or imagine, according to his power that is at work within us, to him be glory in the church and in Christ Jesus throughout all generations, for ever and ever! Amen.

—Ephesians 3:15–21

SECTION ONE

The Two
Become One

CHAPTER 1

THE MAKING OF A MARRIAGE

Grow old along with me!
The best is yet to be
The last of life, for which the first was made.
—Robert Browning

AND THEY LIVED HAPPILY EVER after...." How many times have we heard this phrase, from the fairy tales that enchanted us as children to movies like *The Princess Bride* that we watch even as adults. The "happily ever after"—it's what we all long for in our lives: to be happy, to have all of our dreams come true.

As we sit, enthralled, in a darkened movie theater, we watch, in the space of approximately ninety minutes, as two relative strangers who are destined for love, meet, overcome all sorts of obstacles, and ultimately discover their true soul mate. As the final scene fades from the screen, the happy couple is either kissing at the altar, or walking into the sunset, hand in hand—about to begin their blissful life together, their "happily ever after." The credits roll, and our hope and faith in this dream is reinforced once again.

Our culture has romanticized the idea of love, even to the point of selling the idea that "love is magic," that it is something that happens *to you*, rather than something you can create yourself, with God's help. We have begun to believe that if we can just find the right person, we are guaranteed a life of fulfillment beyond our wildest imagination. The reason that it is beyond our imagination is that life after falling in love is seldom shown in the movies. The movie almost always ends just after the two people "fall in love," and the reality of life "ever after" is rarely portrayed.

From the time we first recognize a fascination with the opposite sex, we become saturated with this idealized view of love. When this cultural influence is fueled with the emotional high we all experience at the beginning of a brand-new romantic relationship, it can become an extremely powerful force in our lives.

We all remember the initial intoxication of the first days of "love." What is actually happening is that the body is experiencing very powerful hormonal changes during this time. In fact, work by psychiatrists Michael Liebowitz and Donald Klein has led them to speculate that the release of the molecule phenylethylamine (PEA) in certain regions of the brain is involved in the emotional response that leads to feelings of elation and attraction around a potential mate. This "chemical attraction" literally causes a natural "high," because PEA is an

endogenous form of speed—very powerful but also very decep-
tive, because when you are experiencing this "high," you're
literally being led by your hormones, not by any semblance of
rational thought![1]

So often we use words such as *love sick, in love, smitten,* and
fallen to describe how these hormones cause us to feel, but such
terminology reinforces the idea that something is happening
to us, not that love is something we can create ourselves. This
is the time when love feels easy and natural, and when we are
experiencing these powerful emotions, it is difficult to understand how any problems could ever enter the relationship.

Without realizing it, we are being trained by this wonderful
experience to believe that the *behaviors* of love will be easy, as
long as we continue to have the *feelings* of love. We begin to
believe that if we just find the right level of chemistry with the
right person, we will experience the right feelings, which will
then lead us to behave in the right way. But as this belief begins
to take root in our minds and our hearts, the opposite belief
also gains a footing: that any relationship that is hard or takes
work must be "wrong."

Ultimately, the greatest challenge in a relationship comes
when the positive feelings begin to wane. Studies seem to indi-
cate that each couple will have an average of about eighteen
months of powerful "chemistry" in their relationship.[2] However,
if, during this time, they do not learn the deeper elements of
love, such as: choosing to love, maintaining a commitment,
valuing their differences, learning to communicate effectively,
and utilizing the principles of teamwork—this chemistry will
slowly begin to decrease. And if these deeper components of
love are not implemented within the first eighteen months of
a relationship, couples will be left with the common feeling

that they have "fallen out of love," or even "picked the wrong person." Frightening questions begin to invade the hearts of the once-blissful couple: *How could I have been so wrong about this relationship? Where did it go wrong? What am I supposed to do now?*

Most couples believe that the *behaviors of love* are a natural by-product of the *feelings of love*, but in reality, just the opposite is true. In a mature, committed relationship, the feelings of love are ultimately the by-product of the behaviors of love.

This can seem confusing to many couples, because at the beginning of most relationships, the feelings of love were so strong and played such a significant role in causing the behaviors of love to feel so natural. Have you ever heard any of the following "confessions of love" from your friends—or even out of your own mouth?

- *She is all I ever hoped for!*
- *He is the perfect gentleman.*
- *He makes me feel so alive!*
- *When I am with her, I feel more valuable than I have ever felt before.*
- *He knows just what I need before I even ask.*
- *She listens to me—really listens—for hours at a time.*

Although it all seemed so magical in the beginning, the truth of the matter is that if there had been a serious conflict with our partner on the first date, we wouldn't have had a second date! But because the first date went better than we could have imagined, the match was lit. The second and third dates were even better than the first, and the flame began to burn brighter and brighter. What we fail to realize is that it was actually the "good" behaviors that were taking place in the beginning that fueled our feelings, but they were masked by the "steroid shot" of chemistry that made those beginning behaviors easier to accomplish.

None of this is said to discount the amazing feelings of love that are present at the beginning of a relationship. In fact, God orchestrated this chemistry to help us get a relationship started. But it is up to us to keep the feelings of love going beyond the initial eighteen months and into the stages in most relationships when people begin to get used to each other, and even take each other for granted.

It takes hard work to build the deeper qualities of love during the beginning months of courtship, because we are emotionally intoxicated. We see life through a romantic haze—through "rose-colored glasses," so to speak. We don't clearly see reality, nor do we want to. It is easy to simply enjoy the ride, rather than take advantage of the wonderful experience of courtship, roll up our sleeves, and learn *marriage*. The initial months of courtship can be an exciting and wonderful time, but it can also be wasted—and can even mislead us to believe the lie that "love is magic," and that it takes no effort to sustain. We begin to think there is no need to work at learning marriage or the behaviors of love that will sustain a long-term relationship. Therefore, most couples enter marriage ill-prepared because of this lie that has saturated our culture—and our own hearts and minds.

Several years ago, John and Mary came to us for counseling. When they first began dating, John and Mary had a storybook

Premarital Counseling

In our culture we do a very poor job of preparing couples for marriage. We spend more time learning to drive a car than how to be married. Because of how we have romanticized love, many people don't see the need to learn how to be married through premarital counseling. "After all, if we love each other, what else do we need?" Unfortunately, these couples are making one of the most important decisions in their lives in the midst of the eighteen-month emotional "high" that begins most relationships.

We believe this "high" can be a wonderful blessing from God to cause two people to be drawn to each other. However, we believe this wonderful time is merely a "booster shot" from God to get the relationship going in the right direction. His plan is for couples to take that eighteen months and learn the skills to create a healthy marriage and seek guidance and training. But our culture has made it all seem like magic—if you have the "high," it will all work out wonderfully without effort. Even couples that see the need to develop deeper skills often don't know where to turn.

Therefore, we have developed an intensive twelve-session premarital counseling series that helps couples prepare adequately for the realities of marriage and find the keys to the abundant life that God has designed for our marriages.

More information on this powerful program is available in the back of the book.

romance. They had met in college and fell in love almost immediately. They spent hours together, basking in each other's presence, having the time of their lives. Most of their free waking moments were spent together. They couldn't get enough alone time, it seemed. Their grades suffered somewhat, but they didn't care, because nothing mattered except what they were experiencing when they were together.

John and Mary had heard that some people had troubles in their marriages, but they were convinced that would never happen to them. They simply *knew* their love was different. They had each found the perfect person for them, and they were among the luckiest people in the world. From Mary's perspective, John was the most amazing man she had ever met—he listened to her intently for hours; he did special things for her; he made her feel like a queen.

By the time they entered the counseling process, nearly a decade had passed since John and Mary's initial meeting and attraction for one another. They had been married for nine years and had two children—things had changed significantly. Soon after the wedding, John began to spend a great deal of time outside of the home, investing most of his energy into building his career. Mary began to feel that she was no longer the number-one focus of her husband's heart, and frustration and hurt began to build up inside of her. The couple found themselves constantly arguing over each other's priorities—and over the family finances. Soon these arguments began to spill over into every area of their lives. Eventually they both learned to "wise up" and steer clear of conflict by avoiding any "hot topics" that could lead to an argument.

Although still frustrated, Mary tried to understand the fact that John had to put in a great number of hours at his workplace in order to build a financially secure future for their family. She channeled her own energy into the children, helping them with their homework and school activities, and maintaining the "perfect" home. But it wasn't long before John and Mary began to feel more like roommates than spouses—and the initial feelings of intoxication they had felt for one another seemed like they belonged in another lifetime. They lived under the same roof, were parents of the same children, but they were experiencing no emotional intimacy whatsoever.

In the first counseling session, as Mary began to share her story, she admitted that she didn't "love" John anymore. In fact, she wasn't sure that she ever had loved him at all. In her mind, she had never had the chance to "be her own person," and she wanted that chance now. She needed a break from the relationship—a permanent one. Mary was asking for a divorce.

When questioned, Mary justified her decision. She was sure that God wanted her to be happy, and she was certain that she could never feel toward John the way she wanted to feel about a spouse. Of course, she still cared about John and his well-being, and she certainly felt bad for their children, but she truly believed that it would be best for everyone if she and John parted ways. "Even John will ultimately be happier this way," she contended.

Mary had bought into the lie of the fantasy of romanticized love. Her romance had lost its magic; therefore she believed that something was terribly wrong. As she thought back over the relationship, Mary became convinced that she and John had gotten married too early, and that she must have simply "picked the wrong person." Perhaps most difficult of all to deal with, Mary longed to experience again the powerful feelings of "chemistry" she had initially felt with John. But in her mind, that could only take place with a new person—the "right" person.

George and Kathy were approaching their twenty-fifth wedding anniversary. Their two children were grown and out of the home. George was a successful professional, and although Kathy had stayed home with the children when they were young, in recent years, she had begun to pursue her own career.

George and Kathy first came to counseling when Kathy discovered that George had become close friends with a female coworker. He reported that although the relationship had not yet become sexual, his feelings were very strong for his new friend; she had sparked emotions in his heart that had "never been touched before." In fact, because of the powerful chemistry involved in this new relationship, he was beginning to question whether he and Kathy were ever really meant for each other.

George wanted some time to "check out" his feelings, but in the meantime, he didn't want anyone telling him what to do. At that point, he wasn't sure he ever really loved Kathy, but he was sure that there was something missing in their relationship, something that could be found with his new friend.

It came as no surprise that Kathy was devastated by George's announcement. During the session, she began to cry as she recounted the many sacrifices they had made for the children, and how much she had looked forward to this time in their life when they could enjoy each other and spend meaningful time with each other again. Although she had longed for a closer marriage as the years went by, she assumed that their life was typical, that they were simply experiencing what all couples with children experience, and that things would improve when their kids grew up and left home.

Unfortunately, during the busy years of career-building and child-raising, George and Kathy's marriage had begun to deteriorate. They had unintentionally neglected to put in the effort that it takes to foster a loving, maturing long-term relationship. And at some point, George fell prey to the lie of the fantasy of romanticized love, and he had become trapped in what we call "the 90-10 Lie."

The 90-10 Lie

In the courtship phase, we become attracted to a person who seems to meet so many desires that we have for our mate-to-be. But when we marry that person, we fail to realize that no one person can meet 100 percent of our needs, and as life goes on, we begin to discover that there are some qualities that our partner doesn't have. Before we know it, we find ourselves attracted to these qualities—in people other than our spouse—and the 90-10 Lie begins to take effect.

The 90-10 Lie states that although we may have 90 percent of our desires met in our spouse, we remain susceptible to the 10 percent of our needs and desires that they do not meet, but that we see could be met in another person. Unfortunately, that 10 percent seems very powerful when we experience it in another person, because we have not experienced it with our spouse before. It resonates as an unmet need that suddenly has the potential of being met, and because the grass is always greener on the other side of the fence, we begin to believe we *have* to experience *those very qualities* in order to be happy.

As George allowed himself to enjoy the 10 percent he experienced with his coworker, he became enamored with the feeling of a previously unmet need suddenly being met. And this good feeling caused him to question the 90 percent satisfaction that he had experienced with his wife for twenty five years. The challenge is that a 10 percent unmet need feels much more significant than 10 percent to the person at the time. George would have denied it was only 10 percent at the time and said it was more like 50 or 60 percent. As a result, he made the decision to pursue the woman with the 10 percent; only later did he realize that he would never have a 90-percent relationship with this new friend. At that point, it was almost too late to turn back and reconcile with his wife because of the damage that his fantasy had created.

All marriages have been affected in some way by the 90-10 Lie, but these effects actually run along a continuum. For many marriages, the effects are on a relatively low level. For example, one spouse may mentally criticize his spouse for not meeting the final 10 percent of his desires, while for other couples, one partner may fall for the lie—hook, line, and sinker—and actually leave her spouse to pursue the "greener pastures." All of these effects, no matter how dramatic, are damaging; a lie is a lie! The 90-10 Lie is destructive, no matter what the effects. No single human being can meet all of our needs, because no one is to replace God in our lives. If we look to other people who seem to have what we feel we are missing in our marriages, then we are buying into the lie—and it will begin to erode our relationship without our even being consciously aware of it.

The Bible warns us to be on our guard against our enemy, who would seek to destroy our marriages—and our lives:

> *Be self-controlled and alert. Your enemy the devil prowls around like a roaring lion looking for someone to devour. Resist him, standing firm in the faith....*
>
> —1 Peter 5:8–9

The truth, not a lie, will set us free:

> *Jesus said, "If you hold to my teaching, you are really my disciples. Then you will know the truth, and the truth will set you free."*
>
> —John 8:31–32

In the following chapters, we will take a look at how this fantasy of romantic love convinces us that love is magic, that it is something that happens *to* us rather than something that we *make happen* ourselves with the help and guidance of the Holy Spirit. We will also see how this lie breaks down the fiber of relationships each and every day. The 90-10 Lie is counter to the truth that love is a choice, an action word, a commitment, and that the feelings of love are a by-product of the behaviors of love.

A loving marriage is something that is *made*. In *The Making of a Marriage*, you will discover that a relationship can be built—or rebuilt—on truth, which creates a solid foundation that will help you reach the full potential of your marriage. You will begin to understand the amazing phenomenon of being attracted to a person who is actually the opposite of yourself in many ways. These differences were designed to be the greatest strength of your marriage, but if they are not managed properly, they can become the source of the greatest conflict. This book will help you learn to speak each other's language more clearly and allow you to make your differences become your greatest strengths. Finally, you will learn the most important life skill any couple can develop: an issue-resolution technique that will enable you to face any conflict or hurt in your marriage, and through the power of teamwork, bring about a win/win solution.

Throughout our years as counselors, we have learned that knowledge and information have to go beyond just being *theory*; they must have *practical application* in order to effect change.

For this reason, you will find practical action steps at the end of each section. These will be essential for you to implement in order to make the changes necessary for a healthy marriage. These action steps will take practice to perfect. But remember, there is a catch in the old adage "practice makes perfect." I (Brent) have played golf since my father taught me at a young age. I have watched men who have played several times a week for forty years or more, but who never seem to improve their game. They certainly got in enough practice, but because their golf swing was bad to start with, they were just practicing a bad swing over and over again. Their practice is not making perfect—it is making it permanent. The only way they will ever get better is to get some coaching and begin to practice more perfectly. Only perfect practice makes perfect. Many of us have practiced unhealthy patterns in our marriages for years. Through these action steps, we hope to help you identify and break these old patterns and begin to practice more perfectly.

Here is the really good news: Old patterns *can* be changed! No matter how many years, or days, you have been stuck in the same ruts in your relationship, you can learn how to interact in a new and more loving way that sparks new life and energy in your marriage. As you read this book, it is our prayer that you will discover God's best for you, your mate, and your lives together in the *making of your marriage*.

CHAPTER 2

POWER-FILLED PARTNERSHIPS: BLENDING DIFFERENCES TO CREATE STRENGTH

Variety's the very Spice of life,
That gives it all its flavour.
—William Cowper

J ASON AND HOLLY BLEW THE top off the romantic courtship chart. Jason not only flew her to a magical paradise island to propose, but he literally delivered flowers to her daily during their entire dating relationship. Holly knew she had the best catch ever, and his pursuit created an effortless response—

giving back to him in romantic home-cooked dinners, prolific praise, and passionate physical affection. Both of them knew they had found the person of their dreams, and they were destined to live happily ever after.

Two short years later, they were in the counseling office hugging the arms of opposite couches with scowls on their faces. Holly exclaimed, "He's changed! He's not the person I married. He faked me out! He was so romantic before we got married, and now I am lucky if he remembers my birthday. We used to have long romantic walks, and now all he does is watch sports and grunt."

"*I* changed?" Jason responded. "What about *her*? She is so critical of everything I do! She used to make the evenings something to look forward to, and now I'm told to warm up hot dogs in the microwave and fold the laundry!"

Jason and Holly are not unusual; they merely bought into the romantic lie of our culture. Our culture has established a philosophy of marriage based on the initial chemistry that most couples feel. Society tells us that love is a feeling; it's an emotion; it's our hearts palpitating; it's getting on board a luxury liner, bumping into someone who, amazingly, uses the same type of breath mint we use, and suddenly falling in love—for the rest of our lives. We then respond on cue—we send flowers, notes, and cards. We look our best and act our best. We become the romantic hero or heroine we've seen in the movies.

Jason and Holly treated each other lovingly because the feelings were so strong, but when they got into the routines of life, their loving behavior stopped, and their feelings began to fade. Eventually they began to resent each other for not being the person they had married. We've taken the chemistry, which God designed to draw us together initially, to be the "end-all, be-all" of our marriages. The truth is, in order to be sustained for a lifetime, emotions follow actions, not the other way around!

So many marriages begin to fail when, six months to a year after the wedding, the "love cloud" begins to dissipate, and suddenly the warm, cozy feelings aren't there anymore. But what couples don't realize is that bit by bit, their actions toward one another have changed—and the feelings are soon to follow. Often a person will notice that his *partner's* actions have changed, and he may even begin to gripe, "Well, you don't do *this* anymore, or *that* anymore," but it's easy to become blinded to the fact that our *own* actions may have become less than desirable. This decline happens so gradually that the effects are not realized until months or years later. We find that the average couple often waits five to seven years after they start seeing some problems before they seek help.[1] By then the patterns are often so ingrained that it is very difficult to change. Marriage takes work—on the part of both husband and wife. But this work, done effectively and with the right focus, brings fulfillment, especially when you understand and apply the principles of marriage—and begin to make them work for you.

The Love Bank

One of the most important principles to learn in marriage is that of the *Love Bank*.[2] Think about your own financial bank account for a moment. On payday, most of us take our paychecks to the bank, make a deposit into our accounts, and then make withdrawals on that account. Some people get into trouble when they try to withdraw more money than they have deposited. Checks begin to bounce; the bank or financial institution starts to assess fees; creditors begin to call. In other words, serious problems occur in your financial life when you try to withdraw more than what you have deposited in your account.

The same is true in the emotional love bank of your marriage. Consider the ebb and flow of the emotions, passion, and love in your marriage—and compare it to the deposits and withdrawals you make in your checking account. If you try to withdraw more, emotionally, from your marriage than you have been willing to deposit, the feelings of love will begin to fall apart. Suddenly you may begin to think, *I don't know what happened! Suddenly he is not attractive to me anymore; I don't like him anymore, much less love him!* Everything the two of you do begins to irritate each other.

We often think that it is the "big" withdrawals from our checking accounts, such as the house or car payment, that break the bank—but have you ever noticed that it's the accumulation of all the smaller, day-to-day purchases that really does the damage? It's the same way with our emotional love banks. Yes, a tragedy or some other difficult situation can take a large chunk of emotion out of the bank, but generally it's the little withdrawals that take place day in and day out that really begin to deplete the account. As you go through the day, not really talking, just going through the motions of your routine, and as you continue to ignore issues as they crop up rather than dealing with them immediately, slowly but surely, the withdrawals are taking place, and before you know it, the love bank is bankrupt.

Unfortunately, just the daily routine of grown-up life is like turning on an emotional vacuum cleaner that can suck the life out of a relationship. Doing the dishes, going to work, paying bills, changing diapers, and cutting the grass all can begin to make withdrawals. These are ordinary activities of life, and they are not bad in and of themselves, but if we don't stay ahead of the withdrawals by making proactive deposits, even the best of relationships begin to suffer.

During courtship, we have what we call a "face-to-face" relationship. We are focused entirely on each other, and we are constantly fanning the flame. We don't really care so much about the rest of the world. But after marriage, we turn and have a more "side-to-side" or "shoulder-to-shoulder" relationship as we begin careers, start families, and build houses and businesses together. Again, this change in focus is not bad, but if we don't have a consistent face-to-face connection and invest in each other, our accounts begin to dry up and our feelings wane.

The good thing is, no matter how low or overdrawn our accounts become, if we understand how this works, we can begin to make deposits today that will replenish our partners' love bank accounts and begin to increase the "returns" of warmth and closeness in our relationships. But how do we make those deposits?

Some of you may insist that you try to do things for your partner all the time, but it doesn't seem to help because they don't seem to appreciate what you do. In his book *The Five Love Languages*, Gary Chapman helps us to see *why* our loving behavior doesn't always do what it is intended to do.[3] Our tendency is to give to others in ways that we ourselves need to be loved.Unfortunately, that isn't always the way our partner needs to receive love in order to really feel loved.

I (Brent) found this out years ago when I planned to do something nice for Janis. I got up early one Saturday morning while she was still in bed and took her car, which had gotten really dirty, down to the car wash. I cleaned the outside, vacuumed the inside really well, and even filled it up with gas, thinking that she would really feel special, and I would be nominated for husband of the year.

I went home, sneaking in very quietly to make sure she still remained sleeping. I was keeping this a secret while waiting for her to go out, later in the day, see her car, and come in the house exclaiming how wonderful a husband I was. A little while later, she got out of bed, and after getting ready, she went out to the garage for something. I just waited for her response as she came back in the house. Surprisingly, she said nothing and evidently didn't even notice what I'd done. I would have to wait to see her response to my loving act.

Soon she decided to go to the grocery store, and I knew the time had come. I was working in the yard when she came back, and I was waiting with baited breath for her proclamation as soon as she pulled into the driveway. But all I heard was, "Honey, can you help me with the groceries?" She never even noticed!

Well, I couldn't let this go by—she needed to know how wonderful I was. (I think I was getting confused about who I had actually done this for!) A week went by, and I had forgotten about it, but soon another Saturday arrived, Janis had another dirty car, and I was going to try this one more time. I went through the same routine, thinking that surely this time she would notice what I'd done and feel loved. I came home and couldn't restrain myself, so I made some noise and woke her up to share the good news about what I had done. Her response on how I had cleaned and detailed her car, to my amazement, was, "Why?" My thought was, *What do you mean, "Why?" It was dirty, and I was trying to be nice!* She went on to ask why

I got up early every Saturday morning and left her alone. Why couldn't I just stay home with her instead of getting so busy?

After saying to God, "What is wrong with this woman You gave to me?" I began to realize that she would rather I just hang out with her in the morning and not get so busy. I quickly had to learn this principle of the love language. My natural love language is *works of service*. One of the ways I love Janis is by doing things for her—washing dishes and performing other chores around the house. Unfortunately, that is not the best way for *her* to feel loved. There are four other love languages, and even though she says she likes all of them, the most important ones for her are *quality time* and *small gifts and gestures*. The other two, *words of affirmation* and *physical touch*, run a close second. The trouble is, the only one I am naturally good at is *works of service*, and I was pretty bad at the other four.

Unfortunately, it doesn't work for us to just say to our spouse, "Sorry, I am not good at those love languages, so you need to learn to feel loved by what is easiest for me to do." If we want our spouses to receive the love we feel in our hearts, we have to learn their languages and make a commitment to learn how we can give to them in the way they receive love. It takes work, but it pays big dividends. The first action step at the end of this chapter will help you put this into play in your marriage and begin to fill up your partner's love bank.

Here is an important point: Marriages don't fail because you married the wrong person; they fail because you have not put enough deposits in the love bank to "cover" the withdrawals you are making! Be clear on this: God created marriage, and He put you and your partner together as a couple for a purpose. There is a destiny in life that He wants you to fulfill. Your marriage was not a mistake! Mistakes may have been made since your wedding day, but those mistakes can be corrected, and with some work, your marriage can become strong and vibrant, the way God intended it to be.

Stranded on the Spaceship!

It's not an accident that you are married to your spouse. We have the wonderful opportunity as humans to choose our marriage partners. Once you have chosen your spouse, God has a unique plan for you and your partner. But marriage can be a lot like being put together with someone else on a space shuttle, heading out to Mars or whatever "planet" God has in mind as the destination. On this mission, God gives each person certain specific tasks to fulfill: for one person it might be measuring oxygen at a certain altitude; for another it might be studying the rocks on the planet Mars. In marriage, it might look like this: One is a planner while one has a more creative flair; one is a talker, while

For Men Only (From Brent)

Men, you know we have a difficult time consistently following through on meeting the emotional and romantic needs of our wives. I believe you love your wife, but you get busy and often forget. Don't let a busy schedule, miscommunication, past failures, or frustration keep you from enjoying the most important and satisfying relationship in your life. Even though your wife knows you love her, she may not always feel like you do. We can help you understand her, demystify her day-to-day romance needs, and get back into what we call a Love Bank surplus.

We have developed a revolutionary way of helping you remember and follow through with meeting her deepest needs. It is called **Mensreminders.com**. See information in the back of the book to begin a new day of connecting with your wife in a way that she will never forget.

the other is a careful listener; one gives emotional detail, while the other is a "just-the-facts" sort of person. Whatever our separate "tasks" are on the journey, we still need our partner in order to fulfill the grander mission itself.

One of the unique phenomena of life is that we tend to marry someone who is our opposite. We have always heard that opposites attract. Of course, during courtship, we don't think this because we are seeing through a romantic haze and only allow ourselves to see the things that make us feel comfortable. But the reality is, as all of us find out in marriage, we probably have many more differences in how we process life and how we behave than we ever thought. If the last thing you would ever want to do is balance the checkbook, you probably were attracted to someone who likes to do that and is good at it. If you are quiet and reserved, you probably were attracted to someone who is more outgoing. It is not a bad thing—it is very good—if we can collaborate together as a team, we will have the best of two worlds in our marriage. We say that if you marry someone just like you, then one of you is unnecessary.

God is creative, and His plan is that you would expand as you get married. The new creation is a blend of the two individuals and has the potential to be more than either could have ever been on his or her own—it is called the power of synergy. The challenge is, back to our spaceships, confined together in such a close space, it's important that we get along with our teammate! Can you imagine being trapped in a space capsule with people whom you couldn't stand to be around?

Marriage is a mission, and God has given you a teammate, a partner, who can help you fulfill your destiny in life. But "being stuck in a confined space" together can become difficult when the differences between you and your partner begin to cause conflict. Ironically, it is these very differences that attracted us to our mates initially. The challenge is that after marriage, it feels as if God placed us into the space capsule of marriage with a complete foreigner. We are different from our partners in so many ways—not just in issues of gender, but also in issues of personality temperaments and life experiences. Many marriages become "proving grounds" in which each partner strives to prove that his or her way is the best way, rather than learning to work together, finding strength in the differences, and using them to complete the mission successfully.

Sometimes the greatest challenge comes when we begin to believe that our part of the mission is more important than our partner's part. Most of the time, when we wake up in the morning, we believe that our way is the right way! Whether it concerns how we roll the toilet paper or how we should spend our tax returns, most of us believe that, no matter what, we are right, and if our spouse disagrees with us, logically, the spouse must be wrong!

The truth is, most of the time, differences are just that: differences. Neither is right, and neither is wrong. God designed us to be different—for a reason. If we begin to see ourselves as two valuable teammates who have been sent on a mission together, we will realize that God wants us to connect in the process, so that we can begin to flow together and fulfill the mission. Our differences will begin to complement each other, our strengths will begin to combine, and we will have "the best of both worlds."

But in our humanness, the process of working together almost inevitably becomes a bit of a challenge. We may bump into each other; we may hurt or harm one another; we may cause each other discomfort. But if we learn how to properly collaborate with one another—as we will discuss in the remainder of this book—we will begin to see the unique benefits that have been given to us in our spouse, and we will eventually gain the full potential of the relationship.

Whether we see these differences as a blessing or a curse depends on our focus. Those things that attracted us to our partner can also become irritations if we don't choose to see them through God's eyes.

Stan and Susan were the ideal couple. Both in their mid-thirties, they met through a church function and were immediately attracted to each other. Susan was a pediatrician who had a great reputation in town for her thoroughness and gentle manner with all her patients. Stan was a corporate attorney who enjoyed his job, but who had many outside interests and hobbies. Susan's serious nature was drawn to the fun-loving, fascinating Stan. Once Stan was interested in anything, he would research it for weeks and dedicate all his extra time and focus on his new project. Stan was attracted to the gentle sweetness of Susan, as well as her dedication to people and the energy that she put into all of her relationships, both personal and professional. Neither had been married before, and they knew that God had saved the very best for them. Their courtship and early marriage was almost like a fairy tale.

I (Brent) met them in the courtship stage, but I began working with them professionally after three years of marriage. Marrying at an older age, Stan and Susan chose to have children immediately. One baby followed another, and they soon had the boy and girl that they had dreamed of. It seemed to be the perfect family. It didn't feel so perfect, however, from the inside. Susan came to me for counseling because she was concerned about the "childishness" that she saw in her husband. He spent too much time and money on hobbies and outside interests. He couldn't seem to settle down and be serious enough. They were adults with responsibilities!

I learned from Stan that he felt trapped, tied down by his marriage. Susan's seriousness had ceased to be a blessing and now felt boring and too negative. The wonderful differences they had seen in each other had become curses. They both felt they had made a terrible error and that somehow they would be better off alone rather than married to this person who was so completely different from themselves.

Neither Stan nor Susan had changed. They were still the same people that they were before they got married. The difference was their focus.

Three Primary Differences in a Marriage

Our focus is most clear when we understand God's design. Human behavior is a very complex thing. Since the beginning of time, mankind has tried to understand why we do what we do. We are certainly not suggesting that we have found all the answers to this question, but in our experience and research, there are three primary areas of difference that combine to make you the unique person that God created you to be: gender, personality temperament, and life experiences. These are also the areas in which we find that we are different from our mates. We'll be covering each of these in the next few chapters, but for now, let's take a brief look at how these areas of difference can affect the marriage relationship.

1. Gender. If you've been married more than, say, two or three hours, you know that the gender differences between a man and a woman are significant, to say the least! Isn't it amazing how much we have in common with our partner *before* we walk down that aisle, and how quickly the differences arise after the honeymoon? We used to like the same kinds of movies, the same music, even the same salad dressing! And we used to think the slight differences we saw between us were "cute" or "charming." However, almost every married couple will come to the day when they look at each other and wonder, *What did I ever think I had in common with this person?* A big part of the problem is that we have married someone of the opposite sex! The differences between men and women are tremendous, and they play a major role in the happiness—or unhappiness—of every marriage.

2. Personality Temperament. All of us have different personality types that seem to be inborn in our makeup. Any parent who has raised more than one child in the same home knows that no matter how similarly you parent your children, their personalities can differ from each other like night and day. Many parents who have a passive child first think that they've got it made, and they consider themselves to be the best parents on earth, dispensing advice to everyone else—until a strong-willed child comes along. Then suddenly they're not the "parenting experts" anymore!

Each of our behaviors can be described by the following four personality types: sanguine, choleric, phlegmatic, or melancholy.[4] Very likely, we won't be *completely* one or the other, but we will have a bent, or tendency, toward one of these four types and an element of a second—a dominant and a secondary. As you interact with your spouse, your personality will play a role in your communication, your issue-resolution skills—your entire relationship. When you begin to understand your own personality, as well as the personality of your partner, you will begin to respect the benefit of your differences and catch the vision of the powerful design God has for this team we call marriage.

3. Life Experiences. The third significant area of differences in marriage stems from our environments—basically, our upbringing, the circumstances in which we have found ourselves, the family system in which we grew up, our birth order, and so on. The conditioning you have received from your environment is extensive—and all of these things have made you into the unique person that you are today.

To understand ourselves and our mates, we need to see the unique combination of these three areas that make us uniquely who we are. We will be limited if we look at just one area. It is the blend of these areas that gives us a clearer picture of why we do what we do—and why our mates do what they do. Marriage requires constant adjustment in blending our unique selves with our partners.

Change *Is* Possible!

Every person—no matter their gender, their personality type, or their life experiences—has the potential for change. Every single person can change—if they want to, and with God's help. But many times, in marriage relationships that have begun to sour, one or the other spouse is working so hard to cause the other person to change, that he or she forgets to work on him or herself! As marriage and family therapists, we have found that if one person in the family system begins to change, the other person or people in the family will begin to change as well, in order to maintain the stability of the system. So, first, begin to focus on how God would want *you* to change in your behavior or your attitude toward your marriage. In reality, you are the only one you actually have the power to change anyway.

No matter what difficulties you may be experiencing, there is always hope and a chance for improvement. The greatest potential strength of your relationship is actually your diversity, for in your differences—whether it be related to your gender, your personality types, or your life experiences—when you begin to come together across those differences, you can have the best of both worlds.

Stronger Than Steel

Although your differences hold the greatest potential strength of your relationship, they also hold the greatest potential for conflict in your marriage. Don't let that deter you from working on the "hot" issues. When you have passed through the fires of conflict, your marriage will have become that much stronger in the process.

We're all familiar with the scripture passage that speaks of the two becoming "one flesh" (Genesis 2:24). Most of us probably heard it recited in our wedding ceremonies, and what we understood it to mean was, "Yes, today we two will become one. Today we are blending our lives together with each other's, and we will be one from this moment forward!" This sounds so beautiful, but soon after the wedding we begin to realize how hard this is to put into practice.

I (Janis) have never been a steelworker, but I do know one or two things about the process of making steel. Steel itself is made up of two very different elements: iron and carbon. Now, iron is strong by itself, but it does not become *refined* and *strengthened to its maximum capacity* until it is blended with carbon; when this happens, the result is high-tempered steel—the strongest type of steel, capable of holding up the incredibly high skyscrapers we see in the skylines of New York City or Chicago.

Now, if you were to take milk and pudding mix and blend them together, there wouldn't be much of a reaction between the two; it doesn't take much energy to stir up a batch of pudding. But neither is the resulting pudding a strong material—it's not capable of holding up much of anything, let alone itself. In order to mix the carbon and iron to create steel, it requires energy, in the form of super-heated temperatures. And the result is something strong, capable of holding together no matter what stress is placed upon it.

Do you understand the analogy? The differences between a husband and wife may be vast, complex, and seemingly insurmountable. They may require a time in the heat, even in the fire, to blend them together in the right way, but the result is nothing short of miraculous—a marriage as strong as steel, capable of holding firm, no matter what stresses are placed on it.

The time of heat, the time of blending, may be uncomfortable, but it doesn't need to be destructive. As you read on, the principles you will glean from this book will help you in turning the heat of your differences into a productive time of blending and strengthening, so that as you come together as one, your marriage will become a power-filled partnership, able to be used for the purposes of God.

The first action step is for both husband and wife to make a list of ten behaviors that, if your partner would do them, would communicate love to you. The love communicating behaviors need to follow the three guidelines in Exercise 1. Exchange the lists, and then each partner should pick one every other day for 21 days and do them. By looking at your partner's list, you will begin to get a picture of his or her primary love language. Begin to pay close attention to the type of things you see on his or her list. The 21 days is to help produce a habit, because it takes three weeks to do so. We are encouraging this to continue after the 21 days, of course, but the first three weeks are to help establish them in your daily pattern to help you get used to the process. This needs to become a lifelong process; the withdrawals of life will continue, and so we must work at staying ahead with the deposits. This initial list will help you get started. Watch for other things you can do that are similar to those on the list and make a mental note for the future. A helpful strategy is to make new lists monthly.

If there is something on your spouse's list you are not comfortable doing right now, just skip it and do the others. Try to use as much variety as possible. Pay attention to your actions. Even if your spouse forgets, you do yours. When you do something, it will be a good reminder for him or her to reciprocate. Of course, this will feel like an exercise for a while. But if both of you keep it going for weeks and months, you will begin to sense that your partner really cares and is committed to loving you in ways that speak your language.

Teamwork Building Exercise 1

Make a list of ten behaviors that, if your partner were to do, would communicate to you that he or she loves you. Make sure that they follow these guidelines:

- *Practical:* They need to be behaviorally specific. Your partner should already have the ability to do these; it should only require his or her decision.
- *Positive:* Do not put down things that you want them to *stop* doing. No negatives—positive behaviors only!
- *Personal:* The behaviors should be directed toward you personally.

1. _____

2. _____

3. _____

4. _____

5. _____

6. _____

7. _____

8. _____

9. _____

10. _____

See the "Love Nugget Ideas" page for ideas. For the next 21 days, pick one of your partner's nuggets and do it for them; average about one every other day.

Love Nugget Ideas

Simple ideas that show me love: Practical, Positive, and Personal.

1. Write me a love note and leave it for me.
2. Go for a walk with me.
3. Rent a romantic/action adventure movie and watch it with me.
4. Bring me coffee or juice in bed.
5. Bring the paper to me.
6. Rub my back (with no strings attached).
7. Pull the sports page out and set it on the breakfast table for me.
8. Prepare a bubble bath for me.
9. Set up a surprise morning of golf with my friends.
10. Surprise me with a cup of tea when I am working at night.
11. Put my towel in the dryer to warm while I am in the shower.
12. Buy my favorite coffee for me.
13. Play a board game with me.
14. Get me a single rose or grocery store bouquet.
15. Rub my back (with strings attached).
16. Drop by my office with my favorite specialty coffee or drink.
17. Make me my favorite snack while I am watching sports.
18. Iron my shirt for me in the morning.
19. Make my favorite meal or dessert for me.
20. Bring me a big glass of lemonade while I am working in the yard.
21. Pick out some simple jewelry and surprise me with it.
22. Mail me a love letter.
23. E-mail me and tell me why you love me.
24. Tell me I look nice and you are attracted to me.
25. Encourage me to have a guy's movie night out.

SECTION TWO

Vivá la
Difference!

CHAPTER 3

MALE AND FEMALE DIFFERENCES

Blessings are found only where
male and female are together.
—The Talmud

J OHN AND CATHERINE HAD BEEN married for thirty years.
One day a friend of John's came over to their house, and
as the two men talked in the driveway, John called into
the house to Catherine, "Hon, can you bring out our wedding
pictures? I want to show Mike something."

Catherine beamed with pride. *Isn't that sweet?* she thought.
*John's going to show Mike how beautiful our wedding was—how
gorgeous my dress was...and those flowers!* Catherine rushed to
retrieve the wedding album from its place of honor in their
living room.

As she walked outside and carefully handed the pictures to her husband, John eagerly snatched the book from her hands. Flipping frantically through the pages, he finally found what he was searching for.

"Look here!" he cried, and Mike leaned in to scrutinize the chosen photograph. "I told you! You can see the '65 Mustang right here behind Catherine. That's the car I was driving back then... Can you believe it?"

Can you relate to Catherine's disappointment when she realized her husband was more interested in his old car than in their wedding day? Or do you more relate to John's excitement over the shining vehicle of his youth? If you have lived on Planet Earth for any length of time, you have surely noticed that men and women are different! They have different interests and different priorities—completely different ways of looking at the world.

Some people have wondered if these differences are God's idea of a "big joke," sort of like a cosmic April Fool's Day prank. How can the two genders be so completely attracted to each other, but be so drastically different—in just about every area of life? Fortunately, we are here to tell you that God is not up in heaven laughing at you; He's not sitting back on His throne, saying to the angels nearby: "Look at these guys! I've got them so confused—they love each other, and yet they're driving each other crazy. What fun!"

God is a good God, and He loves us more than we could ever imagine. He created us with a purpose—and He has designed men and women, each with their own set of strengths, for a purpose: so that through marriage, each spouse would experience the "best of both worlds." When properly understood and managed, the differences between a husband and a wife can actually become their greatest asset. They can complement each other, bringing strength to the two individuals—and to the family unit as a whole.

Common Differences between Men and Women

So what are some of these differences? Perhaps you've noticed some of these common conflicts that take place in almost all marriages that have lasted longer than, say, three months. Here are a few of the ways Janis and I have seen our differences displayed.

The Remote Control. Ladies, you might not be familiar with this item, but a remote control is a small, black object, usually with a number of little buttons on it that, when pressed, will change the channels or volume or any number of other options on a television set. I (Janis) have seen it frequently attached to Brent's hand, but I rarely get to handle it myself.

Of course, we're poking fun at the men a bit when we say that, but the truth is, many husbands and wives watch television in completely different ways. Have you ever sat down to watch television with each other, and as the man holds the remote in his hand, the channels are continually switched—virtually every thirty seconds? The wife will be thinking, *Wow, that looks interesting. I wonder what will happen next*—and suddenly, it's gone. Again, on the next channel, *Well, okay, I guess I can watch this,* then—whoosh—it's gone too. Men, women don't watch TV like that. Women will typically take the *TV Guide*, choose a program, turn on the TV (sometimes even by hand!), and then sit down and watch the show, commercials and all.

Men are completely different! Men love the technology that enables them to switch channels at the touch of a button. They also are more likely to wonder if they're missing something important on another channel, and their attention isn't held as long by one particular show. We watch TV differently.

Movie Rentals. Have you ever gone to the video-rental store with your spouse and spent an hour trying to agree on one movie to watch? If so, you're not alone! Men and women tend to choose completely different types of movies—and so your best bet might be to have each of you pick one movie and then watch them both together, rather than trying to agree on just one.

The next time you go to rent a movie, notice the two different directions in which men and women walk. Women tend to drift toward the "romance" and "drama" sections—they actually prefer movies that have a plot! (Just kidding. Guy's movies have a plot; it just seems to be the same one in every movie.) Even at the movies, women are more focused on relationships, and they will tend to choose a movie that focuses on this theme: how relationships between different people develop over time, the subtle nuances in the relationship, whether or not the relationship will succeed—you name it, *it probably has something to do with a relationship.*

On the other hand, men tend to drift more toward the "action-adventure" sections of the store. They want a movie that shows a hero who conquers something or someone: The bad guy is demolished, and evil is wiped off the face of the earth. The body count may top one hundred before the final credits roll, but in the end, the good guy has conquered evil, and *a task has been accomplished.*

Sports. These days it seems as if women are more interested in sports than ever before. Some women still don't see the logic in a whole group of sweaty men slamming into each other on a field, all to chase a little piece of pigskin, but more women are beginning to follow certain teams and gain an interest in what is going on in the sports world.

However, if you were to look closely at this phenomenon, you would notice that there has been a major change in sports-casting over the last ten to twenty years. In the "old days," when sportscasters reported on a game, that's all they showed you: the game. You saw guys dribbling a basketball down a court, or the football sailing through the air, and then you saw a list of the scores. But now, when you watch a sports report, so much more information is covered. These days, you will see pictures of a football player with his family, or you will see a basketball player's work with the Muscular Dystrophy Association. The American public has begun to develop *relationships* with their sports figures—and because women are much more relational than men, they are becoming more interested in sports than they had been before.

Men watch sports because they want to see their team conquer another team; women tend to watch sports because they feel a loyalty and a connection with that team or player.

Traveling. Men and women also typically travel quite differently from each other.

When we travel together as a couple, these differences really come out. We have four children, and when we are setting out on a road trip, I (Brent) like to load everything into the van at the crack of dawn. Our trip is already planned out—I know exactly the time we need to leave to be at a certain city by lunchtime, and to another city or landmark by the end of the day. I want to make sure that we are making good time—that's

THE MAKING OF A MARRIAGE

my main objective. We can "have a good time" once we arrive at our destination—but on the way, "making good time" is all that really counts!

Along with that is the idea of passing people on the road. To me, there is something immensely fulfilling about moving into the left lane, slowly sliding around a car, and then sliding back into the right lane in front of them. It's almost as if I've achieved some sort of personal victory. After I've passed someone, I enjoy just subtly glancing in the rearview mirror at them and experiencing that "Gotcha!" feeling. The problem occurs when it's time to take a bathroom break—if I've just passed an entire string of vehicles on the road, it's hard for me to pull off of the Interstate and wait for four children to use the facilities: Those cars are gaining ground, and I certainly don't want them to repass me while I am off of the highway! When it's time to eat, I tend to look for something like the Golden Arches, where we can go through the drive-through, throw the food to the kids in the back seat, and hit the road again: "You can go to the bathroom later, kids! Daddy's got to get back out there and repass everybody!"

Now, Janis looks at a trip in a completely different light. For some strange reason, she sees the journey as a part of the vacation. She wants to have "family time" on the trip—and so when it comes to lunchtime, she's not thrilled about a quick stop at McDonalds. Instead, she's generally got a little picnic in mind—generally at a "scenic overview" that ends up being thirty miles off of the Interstate! (I [Janis] would like to note that this is an extreme exaggeration. It is certainly not over five!) We'll spend what seems like a half an hour just getting to the picnic spot, and then she'll pull out a picnic blanket, set everything out and ask us how we're all liking the trip so far.

We've been married for many years, and so I have learned that Janis does know how to build wonderful family memories for us, and we always have a great time because of the family times that she fosters on our vacations. And as a marriage counselor, I also know this is an important step in building memories for our family, yet all the while, my mind is focused on how much time I'll have to make up to repass all those cars when I get back on the road.

I (Janis) have learned to know that Brent operates best from a schedule, and we have had to learn that our differences in traveling are based on the way that God made us: Men tend to be much more task-oriented, and again, women are much more relationship-oriented. The key has been learning how to respect and blend these two.

Physiological Differences

If you've ever experienced any of these situations in your marriage, you know that the differences between men and women can be frustrating at times—especially if we haven't been given the information necessary to understand one another. The fact is, men and women are different in every single cell of their bodies.[1] Because we are that different—right down to a cellular level—it's no wonder that we think and act so differently from one another. God made men and women differently—so that they could become a blessing to each other, not so that they would drive one another crazy! Let's take a look at some of the physiological differences that cause men and women to be who they are and behave the way they do.

For every 125 males who are conceived in the womb, there are only 100 females conceived. So at the very outset, the men outnumber the women—at least before birth. But for every 105 male babies that are born, 100 female babies are born. So that tells us that there are more male fetuses that are miscarried than females. At birth, the males still outnumber the females, but 33 percent more male babies die in the first year of life than females—and by the time we reach the age of eighteen, we are even: There are 100 males for every 100 females. However, by the time we reach the age of eighty-five, the women are far ahead of the game. For every 100 women, there are only 44 men! One of the primary reasons for the greater longevity of females is that women tend to have a better immune system than men do—which is the way God created women, as they are the ones who must bear the children and keep them safe from disease while they are in the womb.[2]

There are other physical differences: The body of a man holds a gallon and a half of blood, while a woman's body only contains four-fifths of a gallon. A man's heart delivers oxygen 24 percent faster than a woman's—and therefore, a man has a greater capacity for exercise and physical labor. Men also have one million more red blood cells in every drop of blood than women have, again providing them with a greater energy potential. On the other hand, while women are more sensitive to pain, they have a higher threshold for pain. If men and women were to run longer marathons, after about a hundred miles, women might start winning, because they have a much higher ability to handle physical pain than men do.[3] (This is especially helpful during childbirth!)

Men have 50 percent more brute strength than women do. They tend to be more muscular—but women have an "insulating" layer of fat cells, which makes it easier for women to gain weight and harder for them to lose those pounds once they've gained them.[4]

A woman's thyroid is larger and much more active than a man's; this causes a woman to have smoother skin with less body hair, and it provides her with many of the elements we associate with feminine beauty. However, the hormones secreted by the thyroid cause women to be more emotional than men; women are more apt to cry—and to laugh—more easily.[5]

Men's heart rates are, on average, eight points lower than women's, but a woman's blood pressure is about ten points lower than a man's. Men also have thicker bones than women do.[6]

Women generally have better hearing than men do, which makes it more likely that they will be sensitive to the tone of a person's voice, even more so than the actual words that are spoken. Have you ever heard a woman say, "Stop yelling at me!" but the man had no idea he was even raising his voice? Women have much more sensitive hearing than men do.[7]

Men and women also remember things differently. A man will remember something if it directly relates to what he finds important, but a woman can remember a tremendous number of details that might not be specifically related to her or her life. This is why a woman can often remember what she was wearing at a party five years earlier, but a man might not even remember that he was there! This is because the memory centers of men and women are organized differently—women can remember details without needing them to relate to a specific pattern, but men must fit the details into a pattern or their brains will tell them that it's not important for them to retain that particular piece of information.[8] This is why your twelve-year-old son can remember the height and weight of all his favorite NBA players, but he doesn't have a clue where his backpack is located!

It's a "Brain Thing"

Despite all of these differences—and many others too numerous to list in this book—the most significant difference between men and women resides in that most important organ of all: the brain.

Brains of men and women develop very differently almost from the moment of conception. When a male baby is developing in the womb, at between eighteen and twenty-six weeks, testosterone and other male hormones begin to interact with the mother, and something very significant begins to take place in the developing brain. The connecting tissues between the right and left hemispheres of the brain, called the corpus callosum, are what allow the two hemispheres to communicate with each other. But during this bathing in male hormones, the corpus callosum begins to disintegrate and becomes smaller in size.[9]

What is the result of this disintegration? Ultimately, it doesn't allow the two hemispheres of a male's brain to integrate information as easily, and therefore they become more unilateral in their thinking. They either tend to be operating in the left hemisphere, or in the right hemisphere, but rarely in both hemispheres at the same time.

On the other hand, because the female corpus callosum remains intact, a woman can easily move in her thinking from one side of her brain to the other. The fact remains that for the most part, men function more in the left side of the brain, and women function in the right side. But women have an easier time moving back and forth between the two.

The left side of the brain, where a man generally spends the majority of his time, houses the logic and reasoning centers of the mind. Eighty to 85 percent of the male population is left-brain dominant and tends to operate with logic and reason paramount in their decision-making processes. This is why men are much more *task-focused* than women.[10]

Because women function with both sides of their brains actively involved in the process, the phenomenon of "women's intuition" comes into play. While dealing with something in a logical sense, a woman can "tune in" to the right side of her brain, and pick up on things that might otherwise be missed. This is what takes place when a woman says, "You know, I'm just getting a feeling about this." Our society has tended to downplay women's intuition, thinking that females are just being temperamental, or even strange, for relying on their "gut instincts." But what we haven't realized is that this is a physical phenomenon: Women, even while processing something logically, are tapping into the right sides of their brains, the centers of emotion, feeling, aesthetics, and social relationships.

Which Machine Are You?

God has designed men and women to operate differently—for a purpose. He wants us to work together to meet different needs and collaborate with each other to get the best of both worlds and be the most effective we can be on this earth.

Dr. Donald Joy compares men and women to two different types of machines: an old-fashioned adding machine and a computer.[11]

A man's brain operates a bit like the old-fashioned adding machine. Do you remember those pieces of equipment? They were rather large and cumbersome, and they took up a lot of space on the desk. Most of them had a big lever on the side and huge buttons on the top. You would punch in the numbers on the buttons, pull the lever, and *voilá!* The adding-machine tape would come out of the top with the correct calculation. This method was a little slower and a little more methodical, but in the end, you could physically pull off the piece of tape and say, "I have got the answer!" If necessary, you could point to all of the different calculations recorded on the tape to demonstrate exactly how you logically reached the correct answer.

Chances are, we don't need to tell you that a woman does *not* operate like one of these old-fashioned adding machines. Rather, her brain operates more like a computer: You punch something in, and you may not understand what all is going on inside of the computer, but almost instantly the right response will show up on the screen. It's a very quick process, one which can be very confusing to someone with an adding-machine mindset, because it can't be explained, and it may not make sense—but it is no less a right answer than the answer determined by the adding machine.

The Best of Both Worlds

As we have said before, God has given men and women to each other to enhance one another—so that we can experience the best of both worlds. Jesus recognized this—and He used both left-brain logic and right-brain emotion when teaching His disciples. The New Testament is filled with parables, stories Jesus told to make a point. The stories themselves tapped into the right brains of His listeners because they created a picture, but the lessons they taught were absorbed by the left brain. Why did Jesus do this? Not because one way was better than the other way—but so that the majority of the people could be reached.

If we begin to vie for power, if we begin to think that our way of thinking is better than our partner's, we are going to experience a great deal of conflict in our world. But if we can begin to recognize the value and legitimacy of our partners, we can take our differences, blend them together, and create a strong, united marriage that contains the "best of both worlds."

I (Brent) am so thankful that Janis is more relational. If it were up to me to raise our kids alone, I would be like the father in *The Sound of Music*—you know, the guy who dresses his kids in their uniforms, blows his whistle and keeps them all in line! I would constantly be asking, "Did you get your homework done?" or "Did you make your bed?"—in other words, "Have you completed all of the tasks and the functions of life?" Thank goodness that Janis can come along and look to the emotional needs of our children, nurturing them and caring for them as only a mother can. God has designed us this way, so that our kids can have the best of both worlds—so that they can grow up both disciplined and loved, both responsible and cherished.

The greatest strength of a male is his ability to get a task done—even if he doesn't feel like it. This is why a man can work in a cubicle, in a job he doesn't particularly enjoy, but is committed to doing it in order to make sure that his family's needs are met. Just fulfilling a task will give a man a strong sense of self worth. Without a job, a hobby, or a ministry on which to focus, a man will suffer from a lack of purpose—but if a man is going to get out of balance, he will likely become overly performance-oriented, driven by the tasks of life.

In contrast, the greatest strength of a female is her ability to see what needs to be done in order to make a relationship better. She more naturally has a sense of what is needed in order to improve the life of the family: Maybe her husband could be reading books to the children, or there may be a need for a family getaway. A woman will draw a large part of her self-esteem from the relationships that she has with other people, and most especially with her husband. She may be advancing rapidly at the office or otherwise making great strides in her career, but if her relationships are not going well, a woman will tend to be depressed, frustrated, and dissatisfied with life.

A man's natural ability to separate himself from his feelings in order to accomplish a difficult task can be a great strength in many circumstances, but it also can create challenges in building relationships. Relationship skills, which are more natural for a woman, are a learned skill for most men. On the other hand, combining the natural built-in relationship manuals that seem to come standard in women with a man's resolution to follow through relentlessly with a task can create a great marriage and family. What a great package God has designed!

As we said initially, human behavior is a very complex process and cannot be described completely in one setting. These characteristics are generalities that are seen predominantly in our culture, but there is a wide variety of types of men and women. That is why we will look in the next few chapters at the other two areas of difference—personality and environment—in order to more fully understand each person. However, some of you may find yourself not fitting even these broad descriptions of male and female. This may cause some to question, "Is there something wrong with me?" Absolutely not! God has made you the person you are, for a unique reason. We have said that about 85 percent of the male population is more left-brain dominant, so that leaves 15% more right brain dominant. They may be more sensitive emotionally, more artistic, and more communicative. These men bring very valuable elements to our culture, and without them we would be lacking. Interestingly enough, they tend to be attracted to a woman who may express more left-brain behavior. "Opposites still attract" is the phenomenon, and it is still critical for each of us to learn to value the differences in our partners to be able to build the most effective teamwork in our marriage.

Isn't it incredible how God designed us and put us together in the marriage relationship? Begin to value your spouse for what he or she brings to your life. As you continue to recognize the significance and value of your mate—including the way he or she thinks and views the world—you will begin to walk in unity and fulfill the destiny that God has for your lives.

The action step for this chapter is to think of five qualities of your partner's gender, based on this information, which you believe he or she brings to your relationship. Write these down on a card and carry them with you for 21 days. Each day, read through this list with a thankful heart. Anytime you see your partner display any of these characteristics, verbally encourage him or her and tell him or her that you appreciate that particular quality. See how your attitude towards your partner begins to adjust.

Teamwork Building Exercise 2

_____
(spouse's name)
Is Made in the Image of God.

Five qualities that are a benefit of my partner's gender:

1. _____

2. _____

3. _____

4. _____

5. _____

CHAPTER 4

THE IMPACT OF PERSONALITY TEMPERAMENTS

If you have anything really valuable to contribute to the world, it will come through the expression of your own personality, that single spark of divinity that sets you off and makes you different from every other living creature.
—*Bruce Barton*

I T TAKES ALL KINDS OF people to make a world." Have you ever heard that statement—or had it quoted to you at an opportune moment? When this statement is made, it's generally because someone has done something strange or even unusual—or even just different from another person's point of view. Maybe it's a man throwing up his arms and singing at the top of his lungs as he walks through a park. Or perhaps it's a woman who meticulously counts her change twice at the grocery store. Or someone who prefers to ride a bicycle to work rather than drive a car. What a boring world this would be if we were all alike! God made us different for a reason; we are all unique because of His design. And He has brought you together with your spouse—someone who, chances are, is a great deal different from you—to fulfill His purposes for your life.

Not only do you differ from your mate because of the gender issues we discussed in the last chapter, but personality differences also play a major role in any marriage relationship. Did you know that a significant amount of your behavior is determined by an inborn personality temperament? This is the second of three major influences that make you who you are. Your personality is like a blueprint that is already in place when you are born—it is a God-given attribute, designed by Him and intended to bring strength and balance into your life, and into your marriage.

The theory of personality temperaments has been around for quite some time. In 450 B.C., Hippocrates, the father of modern medicine, postulated that there were four basic personality types, which were caused by the overabundance or lack of certain "humours," or liquids, in the body. How much bile, blackbile, water, or blood was present or out of balance in a person's body determined whether his personality would be more outgoing (sanguine), more introspective (melancholy), more analytical (phlegmatic), or more assertive (choleric). We have come to understand in modern science that this is not related to bodily fluids, but we can still see that human behavior falls into one of these four categories.[1]

As Hippocrates observed human behavior, he noticed that even at a young age, children of the same gender who are born into the same family displayed remarkably different behavior. If you have more than one child, you probably have noticed that one may have been very quiet and easy as a child. As you watched him in his crib, he just laid there contentedly and cooed. But the next one came along and was remarkably different. Instead of contented coos, you could just see the question in his eyes: "How long is it going to be until I have complete control of this place?" Each person seems to have an inborn combination of two temperament styles that will influence his or her behavior even from the very beginning of life.

In this chapter, we'll take a brief look at these four main personality types, as well as how they interact with each other in the marriage relationship. Although there are many different theories of personality that have been researched throughout the years, we will look at a model we have found to be helpful in understanding relationships. [2]

Which type are you? Which is your spouse? And how can you begin to use your differences to bring strength and a new sense of purpose to your relationship?

The Sanguine: "Let's Have Fun—Right Now!"

Have you ever known anyone whose only goal in life seemed to be to have fun? Chances are, they were a sanguine. The sanguines among us are the popular ones, the "party animals," those people who always seem to be surrounded by friends, fun, and excitement. Sanguines live in the present; they're very exciting, and they have appealing personalities. Sanguines tend to be very talkative, and they like to physically touch and hold on to other people. Sanguines are great storytellers—they talk with their hands and inject a lot of emotion and excitement into any story they tell.

Here are some further characteristics of sanguines:

- demonstrative
- emotional
- enthusiastic
- bubbly
- energetic
- changeable
- idea-generators
- charming
- flashy
- friendly
- sincere
- great at sales

Sanguines almost always have a great many friends—they love people, and people love them.

Despite all of the warm feelings and fun times that sanguines tend to generate, they do have certain weaknesses inherent in their personality. They can be compulsive talkers; they tend to exaggerate, and even tell too many stories, often without enough discretion.

Sanguines can at times "scare off" people who have a quieter, less flamboyant, personality type. Many sanguines have a loud voice—and a loud laugh! They would rather talk and socialize than anything else—and as a consequence, they tend to forget about obligations. They get sidetracked very easily, and their priorities are often out of balance—a lot like their checkbooks!

One great scriptural example of a sanguine personality is Peter, Jesus' most enthusiastic, even brash, follower. Peter was the only one to step out onto the waves and walk on the water toward Jesus. In the Garden of Gethsemane, when the soldiers came to arrest Jesus, Peter drew his sword and cut off one of the ears of the guards. In perhaps the most poignant example in Scripture of a sanguine's living only "for the now," Peter denied knowing Jesus three times after His arrest. This disciple made many mistakes, often because he was letting his personality dictate his actions, but when the Holy Spirit came in and began to control his life, Jesus called this rash and impulsive fisherman, the Rock on which He would build His church. What a redeeming God we have! Only God can take a sanguine and create a "rock" of stability—when we yield our hearts and our personalities to Him.

God's Gift to Each Other

Between the two of us, Janis is definitely the sanguine—and thankfully, we have learned to live with each other's differences. But when we were first dating, back in college, we had a huge struggle as we tried to merge these differences. One of the biggest challenges we had, ironically, was in our spiritual life. After a date, we would often head back to the dorm and spend some time praying together before we went our separate ways. What was supposed to have been one of the most intimate, special times of our relationship, however, was almost destroyed because of how I (Brent) began to perceive Janis's method of praying.

Being a sanguine, Janis was much more demonstrative than I am—hand gestures, emotion, you name it; for me to pray in this way, I would have to be "hyping it up" a bit, praying in a way that I didn't really feel on the inside. But my mistake lay in the fact that I began to project my own personality type onto Janis, and I made the assumption that she must be hyping it up, acting out fake emotions, as well. Pretty soon, I started to view her negatively during our prayer times, and I began to criticize her, even sharply—when all the while, she was as sincere as she could be.

It wasn't long before the Lord yanked my chain and began to challenge me, saying, *Wait a second! Look at who this person is. I have given her to you as a gift—to make your life more fun!* In that moment, I realized that the qualities Janis had that were bothering me, were the very characteristics that God had brought to me in her in order to help bring some balance to my life. *In other words, our differences, when viewed correctly, could be used to strengthen our relationship—not destroy it.*

The Melancholy: "Let's Do Things the Right Way"

Sanguines may be the life of the party, but when it comes to balancing the checkbook, they are not always a paragon of accuracy! Fortunately, the melancholies among us are willing, ready, and able to balance the checkbook—to the penny. Melancholy personalities seek for perfection in everything they do.

The melancholy person is usually deep and thoughtful, introspective, with very high standards for themselves and others. If they don't think they can do something perfectly the first time around, they are not likely to even try it—so at times, they lack motivation. But they have been called "genius-prone"—they are the deep thinkers among us, the idealists, the ones with a purpose to everything that they do.

Other characteristics of the melancholy personality type include:

- ❧ serious
- ❧ purposeful
- ❧ philosophical
- ❧ poetic
- ❧ self-sacrificing
- ❧ organized

We need the melancholies! They are the ones who keep us on task, on target, and on time. But there are also some weaknesses associated with the melancholy temperament—weaknesses that need to be tempered by the Holy Spirit in order for God's purposes to be fully achieved in the melancholy's life. It's because of these weaknesses that the term *melancholy* tends to be viewed in a negative light: People with this personality type do tend to be negative about life, moody, and depressed. They are often off "in another world," thinking about the "bigger issues" of life. Frequently insecure and unsure of themselves in social situations, they tend to be critical of others, unforgiving, and skeptical of compliments—primarily because of their interest in doing things *the right way.*

But these weaknesses don't have to control the melancholy personality. In the Bible, Moses, a classic melancholy, completed a great task—leading the children of Israel out of bondage in Egypt and toward the Promised Land. However, he fought against the idea at first, explaining to God why he wasn't outgoing enough to do this momumental task. He suggested his brother, Aaron, who was a much better communicator. Melancholies can be leaders, but they tend to be reluctant in assuming that role. Moses was sensitive toward the heart of God and His people, organized, and structured, and because of that, he was able to fulfill the destiny that God set out for him, and for which he had been given the precise personality to accomplish.

It's All About Focus

One of the ways that my (Brent) melancholy temperament displays itself is that I tend to be a "neat nut." I feel more comfortable when everything is in its place. This came out early in our marriage when we were trying to share a walk-in closet in our first apartment. When I put stuff on my side, it had to be organized according to type of clothes, color, etc. Janis's idea of a closet was a place to hide things away instead of a showplace. Unfortunately, I thought that my way was right, and I tried to fix her so she would do it "right" also. My approach was poor in that I would drop subtle, critical hints to try to get her to change. One day I even went in to her side of the closet while she was out and "fixed it." When she arrived home, I took her by the hand and showed her how to do it the correct way. Obviously this was hurtful to her, and she began to pull away emotionally because she felt judged and condemned. Our relationship was eroding over a closet.

If I could put into words what I felt the Holy Spirit said to me once I "got it," it would be: "Brent, you need Janis. She will help you learn how to slow down and enjoy life. At your pace, you will burn out quickly. Everything can't be perfect, and even if you got it perfect, it won't stay that way. Look at the blessing of her more relaxed attitude about things, and learn." I felt like He flashed before my eyes the wonder of who she was and all the characteristics she had that I was drawn to in the beginning—her spontaneity, fun-loving nature, creativity, life-of-the-party personality, and confidence. On and on the list went. Well, I finally got the message, and an interesting thing happened. As

I started to focus on the positive parts of her personality, the closet became a very insignificant thing.

I (Janis) began to see Brent become more encouraging and less critical, and it cleared the way for me to see the things in his personality that were beneficial. He never had to search for his shoes in the closet or look for his car keys. At tax time, he would go to one file and pull all the needed information for the accountant. Who knows where it would all have been if I had been keeping all the receipts? We began to see each other's strengths again, and as we both began to learn from the strengths of our partner, the power of teamwork really began to come into focus for us.

Today we are still very different, but we have blended our strengths and even learned how to adopt some of our partner's strengths. Does it mean that by looking in a more focused way on their strengths, nothing they do bothers us anymore? Definitely not, but our attitudes are different. Instead of thinking, *There is something wrong with you; you are broken and need to get fixed,* we say, "Hon, there is something that is bugging me. Can we talk about it and see what we can do about it?" It is all about focus.

The Choleric: "Let's Do Things My Way!"

Cholerics are stand-out kind of people. They are the "movers and shakers"—the leaders, the builders, the drivers in society. These people are dynamic and active—they are always on the move, and they have an almost compulsive need for change.

One of our daughters began to demonstrate her choleric personality when she was just three years old. She would wedge herself behind her dresser and push it out from the wall with her back, just to try to rearrange her furniture. She could not stand to have her room in the same arrangement for very long, because of her choleric temperament—her compulsive need to change things around.

Cholerics are the workaholics, the ones who rise to the top of the organization. People with a choleric temperament are such born leaders that they can move from one organization to another, companies that are not even related in any way, and still rise to the top because of their natural leadership skills.

Other personality characteristics of the choleric temperament include:

- Confident
- Goal-oriented, often extremely so
- Practical
- Good at delegating
- Determined
- Focused on accomplishment
- Great in emergencies

One interesting characteristic of the choleric is that they are often right. This is simply because they have the ability to separate themselves from emotions, look at all of the facts from a practical standpoint, and make a quick decision. On the other hand, cholerics tend to think that they are *always* right, and unfortunately they often insist on having things done their way.

That's one weakness of a choleric—and it's a difficult one for most spouses to cope with. Many cholerics have "know-it-all" tendencies—and over a long period of time, this characteristic can be trying to live with in a relationship. Cholerics are often bossy, have difficulty relaxing, are sore losers, and have trouble giving compliments. They generally avoid displays of emotion, and they have a very low tolerance for mistakes. They tend to be the most critical of the four personality types—both of others and of themselves.

Cholerics have no need for the details of a situation—they just want the "big picture." In a company, this characteristic is an asset, but in a marriage, it can cause conflict, especially when a mate wants to talk about a problem and the choleric would rather talk about how to *fix* the problem. In addition, cholerics have a very difficult time apologizing for anything they may have done wrong. While cholerics may usually be right, they may also be unpopular.

A great scriptural example of the choleric personality temperament is the apostle Paul. Before his encounter with Christ, Paul was intent on persecuting the Christians—and he was going for it with everything he had. And then Jesus Christ appeared to him, blinded him (temporarily), and knocked him off his donkey—and he made a 180-degree turn in the other direction. But the strength of his personality remained the same. He became the greatest leader and advocate of the Christian faith the early Church had ever seen.

The Phlegmatic: "Let's Keep Things Steady"

Phlegmatics are the good, steady, and dependable people among us. Of the four personality types, they are the "Jack-of-all-trades" because they have so many strengths, but none of them stands out in a dramatic way. A phlegmatic person will generally be low-key, remaining unruffled in the face of crisis or dramatically changing circumstances. This temperament type will be easy-going, relaxed, and patient most of the time. "Ol' Reliable" would be a good nickname, because their greatest goal in life is to *keep things steady*.

Other characteristics of the phlegmatic temperament include:

- quiet
- witty
- often has a dry sense of humor
- satisfied
- competent
- good at administration
- problem-solver
- good under pressure
- easy to get along with
- good listener
- compassionate

The weaknesses of a phlegmatic are what might be expected of such a low-key individual: Phlegmatics often have difficulty getting things done on time. They're less enthusiastic about tasks or events, and they are often fearful and worried about the future. They tend to avoid responsibility, but they do have an inner stubborn streak in them. They can become self-righteous or indifferent, they are very resistant to change, and they usually have great difficulty when it comes to making decisions. In Scripture, the person who most fits the phlegmatic temperament is Abraham. He was easy going and good natured but was often plagued by fear. On two occasions his fear caused him to deny his wife and try to palm her off as his sister to other leaders who he was afraid would kill him and try to marry her because of her beauty. He, however, sought God and believed in God's plan for his life and eventually became the father of the Israelite nation.

Key Statement

Sanguine: "Let's have fun—right now!"

Melancholy: "Let's do it the right way!"

Choleric: "Let's do it my way!"

Phlegmatic: "Let's keep things steady."

Strengths

Sanguine: Fun, popular, talkative, charming, social, emotional, enthusiastic

Melancholy: Sets high standards, idealistic, serious, purposeful, deep, thoughtful, organized

Choleric: Born leaders, powerful, strongwilled, confident, goal-oriented

Phlegmatic: Patient, easy-going, balanced, witty, steady, good listener

Weaknesses

Sanguine: Flighty, easily sidetracked, can be overbearing

Melancholy: Often negative, perfectionist, critical, insecure, unforgiving, skeptical

Choleric: Bossy, workaholic, intolerant, unemotional, demanding

Phlegmatic: Indecisive, unenthusiastic, indifferent, avoid responsibility, fearful

Biblical Example

Sanguine: Peter

Melancholy: Moses

Choleric: Paul

Phlegmatic: Abraham

What's Your Combination?

Have you determined which temperament best describes your personality? What about your spouse's personality? But did you notice that you probably don't fit neatly into just one category? You may have strong tendencies toward the sanguine temperament, but you may also have several characteristics of a choleric or a melancholy. Each of us has one dominant temperament that shapes our behavior and responses in most situations. But we also have a secondary temperament, which can come out in other situations. The combination of the dominant and the secondary characteristics in your personality is what makes you the unique person that God designed you to be.

Temperament blends can make life really interesting! For instance, I (Brent) am a combination of the melancholy and phlegmatic personality types, and I am incessantly trying to do everything the right way (melancholy). On the other hand, Janis's personality is a combination of choleric and sanguine, which leads her to often say, "I want to do things my way (choleric), and I don't care if it's right or wrong (sanguine)!" We have seen the benefit of all four of these in our life together as we have learned to let each other be exactly who we were designed to be.

As we look at the blend between the dominant and secondary personality types, we also realize that there are times in life when we must display a behavior that is not really natural for us. If we have to, we can all display any of these personality traits. Our jobs may require a certain role from us at times, or our marriage may need us to step out in ways that don't feel natural. However, if we have to act in a certain way that is more typical of another one of the personality types, it will take more energy from us. For instance, if I (Brent) were called on to do door-to-door sales, I could if I had to, but I would be exhausted at the end of the day. For my melancholy tendency to try to be outgoing with strangers all day would wear me out. If I (Janis) were called on to keep the books for an organization, and I were to sit in a cubicle all day and not interact with other people, I could do it and do a good job, but it would drain the life out of me. My choleric and sanguine temperaments need interaction with other people in order to be energized. The wonderful thing about a team is that we can both focus on what we do best and gain strength from each other.

Interestingly, in our experience, about 90 percent of us marry someone who has a *different* dominant personality type from ourselves. It's true that opposites attract! At first, we are attracted to someone who has different strengths than we ourselves have—but over time, in a marriage, these differences can begin to cause a bit of friction. The weaknesses of our partners' personality type begin to be more glaring than the strengths we had first been attracted to—and we begin to wish that they would change. We forget that our spouse is a gift from God, designed just for us to bring balance to our lives. And we begin to ask our spouses to be schizophrenic, in a way—to keep the "good parts" of their personality but lose the "bad parts"—and we lose our appreciation for their unique contribution to the marriage. Not only do we want them to get rid of the "bad parts" of their personality, but we want them to have the "good parts" of ours. We want them to be two different people. We don't get everything in one person; that is why God created marriage—so we can blend together to create strength.

For the 10 percent of couples who marry someone with the same dominant personality type, it doesn't mean that they have made a mistake or something is wrong with them; the conflict will just be different. Because so many of their strengths and weaknesses are the same, they are in danger of lacking balance. Both spouses will be very strong in certain areas but they will both be weak possibly in the same areas. For example, if two sanguines become husband and wife, it is almost certain that their home will be a fun place to live! But it may not be the most productive relationship, either, because there is no other dominant personality type to balance out the weaknesses of the two sanguines. Two cholerics who are both bent on having their own way may have quite a bit of conflict, butting heads at every turn. They need to pay close attention to the Issue Resolution chapter later in this book. Two melancholies may have everything perfect in their lives, with a meticulous home, but they are probably going to need a social chairman to help them have fun and stop and smell the roses. Two phlegmatics are going to wonder what all the discussion is about conflict because they don't have much, both deferring easily to the other's needs to keep the peace, but they may need a yearly motivational seminar to set any goals for the future.

We Need Each Other!

It is not an accident that you have been given the personality temperament that you have—and that your spouse has his or her own personality temperament as well! God gave you your personality for a reason. If you look at an organization, or even a sports team, you can begin to recognize that all four types are needed to cause things to run smoothly. The sanguines are needed to get out there, sell tickets, and get everyone excited by being the cheerleaders in the group. The cholerics are there to delegate the responsibilities and make sure all aspects of the project or the team are being taken care of. The melancholies are needed to balance the budgets, to handle the details, to cross the t's and dot the i's. And the phlegmatics come on board to smooth out the differences in the team, to make sure nobody kills each other in the process of accomplishing the goals.

Just as we can learn to appreciate the differences of other people in the workplace or in other aspects of our lives, how much more must we begin to appreciate the differences we have with our mate. Don't label your partner. Don't put him in a box because "he's a melancholy, and he'll never change." Or complain about your wife: "She's just a sanguine, and she'll always act that way." We must continually praise and encourage the strengths of our spouses, the ones God gave to complement us, and allow God to work on their weaknesses.

As we submit to the Holy Spirit, both in our own lives and in our marriages, amazing things can happen. We will grow more and more into the image and likeness of Christ, and He will make us into the people He has called us to be. The greatest potential strength of your marriage is your diversity! Embrace it, and allow God to make your marriage a beautiful picture of His grace and love.

This action step is designed to help us refocus. Pick ten characteristics from the descriptions of the temperaments, some from your partner's dominant temperament and some from their secondary one. Put them on a card, similar to the following form. Make a commitment to daily read through this list for at least 21 days and think about your spouse and the character of God in them that you were attracted to in the beginning. Each time you see them display one of these characteristics, verbally affirm them and tell them how much you appreciate that characteristic in them. See how your focus begins to change over time.

Teamwork Building Exercise 3

_____
(spouse's name)
Is Made in the Image of God.

The top ten characteristics of my spouse's personality types:

1. _____

2. _____

3. _____

4. _____

5. _____

6. _____

7. _____

8. _____

9. _____

10. _____

CHAPTER 5

YOUR ENVIRONMENT AND YOU

*Take time to gather up the past so that you
will be able to draw from your experiences
and invest them in the future.*
—*Jim Rohn*

J ANIS AND I HAD BEEN married for about two weeks when
we returned from our honeymoon and began to face
reality. We had brand-new college degrees—but no jobs,
and so we were emptying out all of the wedding cards and
envelopes and living off of the wedding cash. We moved into
our first apartment with no furniture; in fact, we were using a
cardboard box as our dining-room table. But believe it or not,
our financial situation was not as challenging as some of the
other issues we began to bump into.

The day we went to the grocery store for the first time as a married couple was an exciting day. We carried all of the grocery bags into our new kitchen, but as we started to put away all of the food, trouble struck. I (Janis) picked up a box of cereal and placed it in a cabinet to the left of the sink—*which, as everyone knows, is the right place for cereal!*

Brent—and, may I add, his entire family—had this mistaken idea that this was *not* where it belonged. Cereal was *always* stored in a cabinet over the *stove*.

"Why are you putting that there?" Brent asked.

"Because that's where it belongs," Janis replied.

"No, it belongs over the stove."

"No, it doesn't! Besides, if you put it over the stove, where will you put the cooking oil?!"

The cereal was just the beginning. Pretty soon, the argument spread to such life-and-death issues as, in which drawer the silverware should be stored, whether or not the dog's dish should be in the kitchen, and whether or not milk would stay good past its expiration date. Fortunately, we have settled most of these arguments, one way or another, and our marriage survived. But the fact is, each of us has been raised in a completely different environment, which has conditioned us in very significant ways. And these environmental factors will affect your marriage in thousands of ways.

Some environmental factors that will play a role in your relationship with your spouse include your birth order (whether you were the oldest child, a middle child, or the "baby" of the family); your family structure (whether your parents remained married, separated, or got divorced; or whether you were even raised in your family of origin); the kind of school you attended; the career you chose; as well as the thousands of ways we learned to do things, ways that become ingrained in us as the "right way to do things."

When you marry someone who comes from a completely different set of environmental factors, clashes of habits and interests are *inevitable*. For many newlywed couples, just knowing that this process is normal can bring an enormous sense of relief. If we don't understand this, we are buying into the "happily-ever-after" mentality, believing that when we find that perfect person, when the relationship is "right," we will *never* have any arguments, disagreements, or harsh words. But that's not what marriage is about! True marriage is not a fairy tale—it takes work and effort and apologies and forgiveness and a whole lot of compromise, especially when it comes to these "environmental factors," such as which way the toilet paper should roll.

Part of the problem we experience in this area comes from our *expectations*. There are thousands of expectations that we have about our marriage, most of which come from the environment in which we were raised as children. These can range from whether or not you should put up a live Christmas tree or a fake one; when you should put up the Christmas tree; as well as all of the other rituals that go with the holiday season. They include our values: what is cheating, and what it is not; is it ever acceptable to tell a lie; how the children will be disciplined—and for what. And they include the thousands of details of our lives: After how many rings should you answer the phone? Should you always go to bed together at the same time? Who is responsible for the cooking, the cleaning, and other household chores?

We once saw a couple in counseling who had been married for over twenty years. The wife had been holding resentment against her husband because he never locked the doors at night. She would wait every night for twenty years for him to go around the house and lock the doors, making sure the house was secure for the night—and he never did it. Finally, she gave up and decided that she would do it, and so she began to go around and lock up the house every night, but she was angry about it. One of her deepest expectations was not being fulfilled.

When we spoke in our counseling session about the issue, we discovered that in her childhood home, her father would lock up the house each night, but in the husband's childhood home, there was no father, and so his mother completed that task at the end of the day. They had never discussed the issue, but each had brought in their expectations from their childhoods—the result of the environment in which they were raised—and the lack of awareness and communication over this issue caused unnecessary pain and distance in their relationship.

"Cutting a Groove"

In our childhoods, there was a sort of "conditioning" that took place in our lives. Certain "grooves" were actually cut into our thinking, and as we experienced life as it was we began to believe, *this is the way life is supposed to happen*. The official term for this is a *schema*—a certain way of thinking, a blueprint of information, a schematic diagram that tells a person "this is how we do things." Most of us develop these schemas in our childhoods, when we are very young. It's even been suggested that an actual groove in the neural pathways of our brains is created and established according to a certain pattern—which means that it is very difficult to alter that pattern to any degree.

A good example of this is riding a bicycle. I (Brent) remember teaching each of my four children how to ride a bike. At first,

I held on to the back of the seat while pushing them along, as they looked back at me with terror in their eyes. Their bodies didn't know how to ride a bicycle yet, so they were very unstable. But as we did it over and over again, their bodies began to send messages to their brains, teaching them how to ride a bike. Their legs, their arms, the balance components in their inner ears, and their eyes were all sending impulses to the brain, which was formatting, like a computer program, "how to ride a bicycle." The more we practiced, the more stable they became. Eventually they didn't need my help and were off riding on their own for hours. All of us had this experience as children, and because of it, even if we haven't ridden a bicycle in years, we could mount one, and after maybe just a moment of instability, we would take right off. Our brain remembers what to do because of the hours of practice we had put in.

This is an example of the wonderful way God made us; it allows us to not have to learn how to talk every day; when we have a hunger pang, we go eat and it keeps us alive; and we can get out of bed each morning and just start walking. The challenge is that we have also learned some behaviors that are not as healthy, but they are also ingrained in our memories. We react the same way our parents or coaches did, even when we don't want to. We carry patterns, or schema, for all types of things from our environment.

All of us can remember experiencing Christmas morning as children. Perhaps you got up early that morning and your family ripped into the presents first thing—even before the sun came up. Or perhaps you opened the presents on Christmas Eve instead of Christmas morning. Perhaps your dad fixed pancakes for everyone. Or perhaps you didn't have breakfast at all, but had a huge dinner in the middle of the afternoon.

How about birthdays? In your family, were birthdays a huge deal—with presents, cake, ice cream, and a party with twenty or more people? Or were they more subdued affairs, with maybe one present and the "Happy Birthday" song? So many couples experience huge misunderstandings when it comes to birthdays or other holidays—all because of unspoken expectations. If one person comes from a family that goes all out in birthday celebrations, but marries a person who considers birthdays to be "no big deal," when the big day rolls around, a huge misunderstanding is almost inevitable. We believe that our way is the way birthdays should be done—that is our schema for birthdays! So many women come to counseling complaining that all their husbands bought them for their birthday was a card—that they handed to them at the end of the day with a mumbled "Happy birthday." Well, part of the problem is that's what they learned birthday celebrations should be, and it may not be a personal insult at all.

The Culture Clash

When two very different people get married—a male and a female, with completely different personalities, and raised in completely different environments—what could be called a "culture clash" takes place. Two cultures come together, and it is inevitable that some sort of conflict will occur. Whose side will win out? Will the cereal be stored over the stove or to the left of the sink?

When the issue becomes "who will win," however, we miss out on the benefits that both perspectives can bring to our relationship. Maybe it's better to store the cereal someplace other than where your family has kept it. You'll never know unless you are willing to compromise.

As a general rule, when people are introduced to new information, such as what occurs in the early days in a marriage, they have one of three common responses.

1. "They don't know what they're talking about!" Some people simply choose to reject the new information, without even considering its value or contribution to their benefit. Have you ever listened to what your spouse had to say—and then immediately dismissed it? This doesn't just happen between newlyweds; older couples have this response too. *He's just crazy. I don't know what's wrong with his family that they would do things that way, but that's not the way it's* supposed *to happen!* This response leaves absolutely no room for compromise and the benefits new ideas can bring.

2. "She doesn't mean it the way she said it," or **"That might have worked for their family, but what I think will work better for us today."** Other people take the new information, and while they "accept" it to a degree, they change it around to fit their own schemas. This response will not lead to any creative teamwork to build the relationship.

3. "Wow, that way of thinking really has some significance. I think we should consider the value of your ideas." The third response, and the one that will bring the best results in your marriage, is that of acceptance. *Acceptance* does not necessarily mean *agreement or approval*; it simply means that you choose to consider the information and the value that it could bring to the situation. This third response is the only way that change can be made in a way that benefits the whole relationship.

It takes a lot of energy to change a pattern, to change the groove, the way of thinking that you've had all your life. Have you ever noticed that even when you determine that you will *not* react a certain way or get angry at your spouse or your children, sometimes you do? When you are tired, when you've had a bad day, or when someone pushes your "hot buttons," do you find that you react in exactly the same way as you always have? It takes energy to change, and it's often the easiest thing in the world to fall back into the grooves that we've had from our past.

Change *is* possible. It is not easy, but it can happen. However, it only happens when we recognize the need for change, are open to other viewpoints, then work together, and practice over and over until change occurs. Sometimes we get so stuck in our patterns that we need the help of a professional counselor to identify and coach us in that process of change. But remember, the human being is very adaptable and has incredible potential for change when the motivation and tools are present.

A Duffle Bag of Issues

Obviously, the best way for us to respond to the differences we experience every day between us and our spouses is the third way—to accept those differences as valid and begin to consider them as important input into our relationship. God has placed us in our particular marriages for a reason—to give us a new perspective, to stretch, grow, and mature us, taking us to new levels in Him. We must make the conscious decision to love—not to *feel* love, but to *love*, to take action to love our partners the way that God would have us love them.

Unfortunately, most of us carry around the issues in our marriage like they are a duffle bag over our shoulders. We like to pull out these issues whenever we need a little ammunition on our side of an argument. A husband may say, "I can't believe you just did that," and the wife may reach into the Duffle Bag of Issues and respond, "Well, that's nothing compared with what you did fifteen years ago!"

We carry around our issues because we never know when we're going to need them. We may think, *He hurt me so much—he doesn't even know how badly he hurt me! He doesn't realize how painful this really is. I'm going to keep bringing it up and bringing it up and bringing it up until he finally recognizes what he's done!* On the other hand, some of us may not even realize that the baggage we're carrying is even affecting us. We may honestly think that the huge argument we've started is about our spouse being ten minutes late, and that it's not linked to twenty-seven years of baggage that we've been hauling around—but if that's the case, chances are, we're living in denial.

If we don't learn to let these things go, then each situation that takes place will gradually become worse. Over and over again, we have seen relationships that have deteriorated so far that it doesn't take much to set off an argument. In the beginning, it really took a lot to cause an argument, but after years of baggage accumulating, all it takes is one wrong look and they are at each other's throats.

When I (Brent) was a little boy, I loved to watch *The Daniel Boone Show*—probably because it was filled with action and adventure. Daniel was a hero and won all the battles, and just like any other little boy (or grown man), I lived vicariously through Daniel's life. In one episode, Daniel Boone or one of his cohorts planned to blow up a fort, and they took one of the kegs of gunpowder out of a storage cabin in the fort, knocked a hole in it, and crept out of the fort and into the woods, trailing the gunpowder all the way. When they had gone far enough into the woods, Daniel Boone fired his musket, setting off a spark that ignited the gunpowder. All of a sudden, the trail of gunpowder flared up, and a line of fire quickly began to snake its way through the woods all the way back to the fort, where all the other kegs of gunpowder were stored. And at that moment, the entire fort spectacularly exploded—flames, smoke, and debris flying everywhere!

While that explosion made for an exiting episode of *The Daniel Boone Show*, it isn't nearly as exciting when it happens in relationships. One little situation, one little spark, may not seem like a big deal, but when there is a trail that leads back to the volatile powder keg of issues—it leads to an explosion far beyond what the situation warrants. Have you ever experienced your partner exploding over something that seemed small at the time, but when you looked at it further, you could see that they weren't reacting to the small situation, but that there were bigger issues at stake? It's a common problem—but one that can be solved. The key is to stay current with our partners by learning to resolve issues effectively (which we will deal with in a future chapter) and to keep the slate clean by living in an attitude of forgiveness.

True Forgiveness

So how do we let go? How can we really forgive each other of past issues and move on?

Most of us approach the idea of forgiveness like our own kids tend to approach it. We can remember a time when the kids were little and got into a squabble. One of them ran into our room and began to whine, "He called me a nerd!" We called the other one into the room and said, "Guys, we don't talk like that. We don't label each other, and we don't call each other names. Now I want you to tell your brother you're sorry."

How did our sweet, precious child apologize to his brother? "I'm sorry you're a nerd!"

Of course, we almost died laughing before we dealt seriously with the situation, but that is not true repentance! Unfortunately, we tend to take the same attitudes with our partners:

- "You know, honey, I just want to tell you that I'm sorry. I'm sorry for putting demands on you that you're just incapable of meeting."
- "I'm sorry I didn't recognize how insensitive you'd be in this situation."
- "I'm sorry that I've stayed in such a miserable relationship for so long, when you obviously can't deal with the things that have been going on."

We say the words "I'm sorry," but we're not repentant. We're simply using these words as a way to manipulate our partner and get our point across in an "acceptable" way. Christians especially are really good at cloaking barbs and insults in "Christianese:" "You know, honey, I just read a scripture and it reminded me of you." Or, "It was revealed to me in prayer that you need to work on your anger problem." God wants us to grow up! Stop pointing the finger at your spouse and begin to truly forgive!

Instead of working on how we need to get our partner to repent, we need to focus on the questions, *What do I need to repent of? What is my responsibility in this particular situation?* You cannot change another person, and you cannot be held responsible for your partner's behavior—but you *are* responsible for your own, including your decision to forgive, or your refusal to do so.

The good news is that when you choose to forgive, when you begin to deal with your own issues, it will have a positive effect on your partner! When you stop trying to be the Holy Spirit in your spouse's life, it frees him or her to hear from the Holy Spirit directly. We need to step back, check our own hearts, and let God deal with our spouse's behavior. We can't fix our partners—but we can forgive them.

So many Christians have a tendency to go through the motions when it comes to forgiveness, but God asks us to truly forgive—from our hearts. Most of the time, we know that we are supposed to forgive, and so we pray, *Lord, I know I need to forgive them, and so, okay, Lord, I forgive them—right* now! We *feel* better—for about five seconds, until the anger we had comes rushing back; then we begin to question whether or not we are doing it right because the "feeling better" part didn't last. We may question ourselves or God about whether or not this "forgiveness thing" really works.

It's important to realize that *true forgiveness is a process*. It's not a one-time, instant event that takes place when you pray a prayer and expect all of the negative feelings to disappear.

"The Magic Eyes: A Little Fable"
The following fable from Lewis Smedes' book, *Forgive and Forget*, demonstrates the power of—and work involved in—true forgiveness.

> *In the village of Faken in innermost Friesland there lived a long thin baker named Fouke, a righteous man, with a long thin chin and a long thin nose. Fouke was so upright that he seemed to spray righteousness from his thin lips over everyone who*

came near him; so the people of Faken preferred to stay away.

Fouke's wife, Hilda, was short and round, her arms were round, her bosom was round, her rump was round. Hilda did not keep people at bay with righteousness; her soft roundness seemed to invite them instead to come close to her in order to share the warm cheer of her open heart.

Hilda respected her righteous husband, and loved him too, as much as he allowed her; but her heart ached for something more from him than his worthy righteousness.

And there, in the bed of her need, lay the seed of sadness.

One morning, having worked since dawn to knead his dough for the ovens, Fouke came home and found a stranger in his bedroom lying on Hilda's round bosom.

Hilda's adultery soon became the talk of the tavern and the scandal of the Faken congregation. Everyone assumed that Fouke would cast Hilda out of his house, so righteous was he. But he surprised everyone by keeping Hilda as his wife, saying he forgave her as the Good Book said he should.

In his heart of hearts, however, Fouke could not forgive Hilda for bringing shame to his name. Whenever he thought about her, his feelings toward her were angry and hard; he despised her as if she were a common whore. When it came right down to it, he hated her for betraying him after he had been so good and so faithful a husband to her.

He only pretended to forgive Hilda so that he could punish her with his righteous mercy.

But Fouke's fakery did not sit well in heaven.

So each time that Fouke would feel his secret hate toward Hilda, an angel came to him and dropped a small pebble, hardly the size of a shirt button, into Fouke's heart. Each time a pebble dropped, Fouke would feel a stab of pain like the pain he felt the moment he came on Hilda feeding her hungry heart from a stranger's larder.

Thus he hated her the more; his hate brought him pain and his pain made him hate.

The pebbles multiplied. And Fouke's heart grew very heavy with the weight of them, so heavy that the top half of his body bent forward so far that he had to strain his neck upward in order to see right. Weary with hurt, Fouke began to wish he were dead.

The angel who dropped the pebbles into his heart came to Fouke one night and told him how he could be healed of his hurt.

There was one remedy, he said, only one, for the hurt of a wounded heart. Fouke would need the miracle of the magic eyes. He would need eyes that could look back to the beginning of his hurt and see his Hilda, not as a wife who betrayed him, but as a weak woman who needed him. Only a new way of looking at things through the magic eyes could heal the hurt flowing from the wounds of yesterday.

Fouke protested. "Nothing can change the past," he said. "Hilda is guilty, a fact that not even an angel can change."

"Yes, poor hurting man, you are right," the angel said. "You cannot change the past; you can only heal the hurt that comes to you from the past. And you can heal it only with the vision of the magic eyes."

"And how can I get your magic eyes?" pouted Fouke.

"Only ask, desiring as you ask, and they will be given you. And each time you see Hilda through your new eyes, one pebble will be lifted from your aching heart."

Fouke could not ask at once, for he had grown to love his hatred. But the pain of his heart finally drove him to want and to ask for the magic eyes that the angel had promised. So he asked. And the angel gave.

Soon Hilda began to change in front of Fouke's eyes, wonderfully and mysteriously. He began to see her as a needy woman who loved him instead of a wicked woman who betrayed him.

The angel kept his promise; he lifted the pebbles from Fouke's heart, one by one, though it took a long time to take them all away. Fouke gradually felt his heart grow lighter; he began to walk straight again, and somehow his nose and his chin seemed less thin and sharp than before. He invited Hilda to come into his heart again, and she came, and together they began again a journey into their second season of humble joy.[1]

Let's look at some of the main points of this story:

1. The one who is hurt the most by unforgiveness is the one who has been offended but who can't release and forgive. Fouke was the one most hurt by his unforgiveness—not Hilda.

2. Your unforgiving heart will not become heavy overnight— but eventually, it will begin to affect your perspective. It took many, many pebbles before Fouke began to stoop under the weight of his heavy heart, but once he became bent over from the unforgiveness he was carrying, it affected his vision. He could no longer stand up straight and look around clearly. He could only see life through one perspective—that of resentment and bitterness.

3. We must begin to see the person who has offended us through God's eyes of forgiveness. Although they are referred to as "magic eyes" in the story, there is no magic involved in true forgiveness—it takes hard work. But when we choose to look at those who have hurt us through God's eyes, we begin to recognize their weaknesses, their insecurities, and their needs—the things that caused them to hurt us in the first place.

Our definition of sin is "an inappropriate response to a real need." We all have legitimate needs in our lives but often don't know how to get them met properly, the way God designed. Unfortunately, this leaves us choosing a counterfeit behavior to try to get our needs met ourselves. This usually is hurtful to someone else. Only when we recognize that people hurt others out of their own hurts and needs can we truly begin to release the offense. This is the beginning of mercy and empathy, two keys to true forgiveness.

4. The journey of forgiveness is a process and will take time to accomplish. In Matthew 18:21–22, when Peter asked if they should forgive someone up to seven times, Jesus responded, "Not seven times, but seventy-seven times." Now, I (Brent) don't believe that means on the 78th time we don't have to forgive any more; it just means forever. It is usually not 77 times we are hurt; it is that we remember it 77 or more times, so forgiveness requires that every time the memory comes back we have a choice to forgive or not. If we choose forgiveness, eventually our hearts will be free to move on to life and liberty.

Practical Solutions

There are a number of tools that we often offer couples who are struggling in the area of forgiveness. First, begin to picture your spouse when he or she was young, especially if you know that he or she went through a traumatic or hurtful situation at a young age. Write out a paragraph of your understanding of your spouse's vulnerability, hurt, and need that you want to be reminded of when you think about him or her. Get a picture of your spouse at that age, attach it to this paragraph, and begin to carry that around with you, especially if you're having a hard time releasing your negative thoughts toward him or her. There's something innocent about the picture of a child. And while we are in no way excusing this person's behavior as an adult, to look at him or her in a previous innocent state, to begin to realize that he or she is human also, and that he or she has experienced hurt, pain, and insecurity can do a world of good in moving a person toward a heart of forgiveness.

Another extremely important and helpful tool is journaling. Sometimes we tell people to go ahead and write out "anger letters" in which they spill out everything negative, everything hateful—all of the venom they have kept bottled up inside. They spill it all out in this letter, which, by the way, is *never* intended to be read by the other person. If we think another person might potentially read what we are writing, we are much more likely to censor our words, and that would defeat the purpose of this exercise. *All* of the hatred and negative feelings need to be dispelled, and then you may either tear up the letter, burn it, or even flush it down the toilet! Do whatever you want with it, but get those feelings out from inside of you and onto paper. It "pulls the plug" on those negative, volatile feelings, and allows the process of forgiveness to begin.

A final tool that can help forgiveness to take place is that of praise and encouragement. By praising and encouraging the positive things that we *do* see in our spouses, we begin to be more aware of the potential for healing and change in the relationship. What are the things that make your spouse special and unique? What attracted you to him or her in the first place? What do you love about your partner?

The environment can be a powerful tool to draw couples together or to pull them apart. It takes the power of forgiveness to overcome the differences between a husband and a wife and to unite them in a marriage that is strong enough to withstand any conflict or pressure that might come.

Teamwork Building Exercise 4

Take a moment and write out an appreciation letter to your mate, completing the following sentences:

"Thank you for the way you always..."

"You are so cute when you..."

"The first thing that attracted me to you was..."

"The thing that I didn't know about you before we were married, but which has pleasantly surprised me is..."

"The qualities in you that I want our children to have are..."

"You make my life better by..."

"The things that physically attract me to you are..."

"The things that I like most about your personality are..."

"Our most special day to me was..."

"If I could give you anything in the world right now, it would be..."

"Thank you for..."

Pick a special time that you can sit and share this with your spouse.

A second exercise is to make a list of four or five qualities that you believe your partner brought to the marriage from his or her background. As you have done in the previous two chapters, write these out in the format as follows. For the next 21 days, read them through daily and verbally affirm your mate. Once again, watch how your focus changes.

Teamwork Building Exercise 5

_____
(spouse's name)
Is Made in the Image of God.

Four strengths that my partner brought into the relationship that came from the influence of his or her family and life experiences include:

1. _____

2. _____

3. _____

4. _____

SECTION THREE

Working It Out

CHAPTER 6

COUPLE COMMUNICATION: SKILLS NEEDED TO SPEAK THE SAME LANGUAGE

Ultimately, the bond of all companionship, whether in marriage or friendship, is conversation.
—Oscar Wilde

A S WE BEGIN TO TALK about the communication issues present in most marriages, let's first tune in to an episode of the weekly radio show, *The Trials of Our Lives.*

Announcer: *Welcome to today's episode of* The Trials of Our Lives. *Today we're featuring Roger and Elaine. Roger is attracted to a woman named Elaine, and when he asks her out to a movie, she accepts. They have a good time and enjoy each other's company, and a few nights later, he asks her out to dinner. Again, they enjoy themselves. They continue to see each other regularly, and after a while they realize that neither of them is seeing anyone else. And then one evening, as they are driving home, a thought occurs to Elaine. And without really thinking about it, she says aloud . . .*

Elaine: ". . . Do you realize that, as of tonight, we've been seeing each other for exactly six months?"

Announcer: *Silence fills the car. To Elaine, it seems like a very loud silence. She begins to think to herself . . .*

Elaine (thinking): ". . . Gee, I wonder if it bothered him that I said that? Maybe he's been feeling confined by this relationship. Maybe he thinks I'm trying to force him into some kind of obligation that he doesn't want or isn't sure of."

Announcer: *And Roger is thinking . . .*

Roger (thinking): ". . . Gosh. It's been six months?"

Announcer: *And Elaine is thinking . . .*

Elaine (thinking): ". . . But, hey, I'm not so sure I want a serious relationship, either. Sometimes I wish I had a little more space, so that I'd have time to think about whether I really want us to keep going the way we are, moving steadily toward . . . where are we going? Are we going to keep seeing each other at this pace? Are we heading toward marriage? Toward children? Toward a lifetime together? Am I really ready for that kind of commitment? Do I even know this person?"

Announcer: *And Roger is thinking . . .*

Roger (thinking): ". . . Six months. Hmph. That means it was about February when we went out, right after I had taken the car in to the dealership, which means—let me check the odometer. Whoa! I'm way overdue for an oil change!"

Announcer: *Meanwhile, Elaine is thinking . . .*

Elaine (thinking): ". . . He's upset! I can see it on his face. Maybe I'm reading this completely wrong. Maybe he *does* want more from our relationship, more intimacy, more commitment. Maybe he has sensed—even before I sensed it—that I was feeling some reservation. Yes, I bet that's it! That's why he's so reluctant to say anything about his own feelings. He's afraid of being rejected."

Announcer: *And Roger is thinking . . .*

Roger (thinking): ". . . I'm going to have them look at the transmission too. I don't care what those morons say, it's still not shifting right. And they'd better not blame it on the cold weather; what are they talking about, cold weather? It's 87 degrees out! This thing is shifting like a garbage truck, and I paid those incompetent thieves six hundred bucks."

Announcer: *And Elaine is thinking . . .*

Elaine (thinking): ". . . He's angry. . . and I don't blame him! I'd be angry too. I feel so guilty putting him through this. But I can't help the way I feel! I'm just not sure. . ."

Announcer: *And Roger is thinking . . .*

Roger (thinking): ". . . They'll probably say it only has a ninety-day warranty. That's exactly what they're going to say, those scumballs!"

Announcer: *And Elaine is thinking . . .*

Elaine (thinking): ". . . Maybe I'm just too idealistic. Waiting for a knight to come riding up on his white horse, when I'm sitting right next to a perfectly good person, a person I truly care about. A person who seems to truly care about me. A person who is in pain because of my self-centered, school-girl fantasy."

Announcer: *And Roger is thinking . . .*

Roger (thinking): ". . . Warranty. They want a warranty? I'll give them a warranty!"

Elaine (aloud): "Roger. . ."

Roger (aloud, and startled): "What?!"

Elaine (aloud, her eyes beginning to brim with tears): "Please don't torture yourself like this. Maybe I should never have said . . . . Oh, I feel so . . ."

Elaine breaks down, sobbing.

Roger (aloud): "What?!?"

Elaine (sobbing): "I'm such a fool! I mean, I know there's no knight, I really know that. It's silly. There's no knight, and there's no horse."

Roger (aloud): "There's no horse?!?"

Elaine (aloud): "You think I'm a fool, don't you?"

Roger (aloud, glad to finally know the right answer): "No!"

Elaine (aloud): "It's just that . . . it's that . . . I need some time . . ."

Announcer: *There is a fifteen-second pause while Roger—thinking as fast as he can—tries to come up with a safe response. Finally, he comes up with one that he thinks might work.*

Roger (aloud): "Yes!"

Elaine (aloud): "Oh, Roger! Do you really feel that way?"

Announcer: *Elaine is deeply moved, and she reaches over and touches Roger's hand.*

Roger (aloud): "What way?"

Elaine (aloud): "That way about time. . . ?"

Roger (aloud and confused): "Oh! . . . Yes!"

Announcer: *Elaine turns to face him and gazes deeply into his eyes, causing him to become very nervous about what she might say next, especially if it involves a horse! At last she speaks.*

Elaine (aloud): "Thank you, Roger!"

Roger (aloud): "No, thank you!"

Announcer: *Roger takes Elaine home, where she lies on her bed a conflicted, tortured soul, awake until dawn. On the other hand, when Roger gets back to his place, he opens a bag of Doritos, turns on the TV, and immediately becomes involved in a rerun of a tennis match between two Czechoslovakians he's never even heard of. A tiny voice in the far recesses of his mind tells him that something major was going on back there in the car, but he's pretty sure that there is no way that he would ever understand what it was. And so, he figures, it's best if he just not think about it. This is also Roger's policy regarding world hunger.*

The next day, Elaine will call her closest girlfriend, or perhaps two of them, and they will discuss the situation for six straight hours. In painstaking detail, they will analyze everything he said and everything she said, going over it time and time again, exploring every word, expression, and gesture for nuances of meaning, considering every possible ramification. They will continue to discuss this subject off and on for weeks, maybe months, never reaching any definite conclusions, but never getting bored with it, either.

Meanwhile, Roger, while playing racquetball one day with a mutual friend of his and Elaine's, will pause just before serving, frown, and say . . .

Roger (aloud): ". . . Bill, did Elaine ever own a horse?"

Announcer: *And thank you for tuning in to today's episode of* The Trials of Our Lives. [1]

It shouldn't take a radio program such as this to convince us that miscommunication between men and women takes place all the time! Obviously, men and women speak two entirely different languages—almost to the point that when you get married, you may suddenly feel like you are living with a foreigner. It's almost as if one of you speaks Chinese and one of you speaks Latin, and if the two of you don't begin to learn some elements of the other person's language system, you will live in a world of miscommunication, hurt feelings, anger, and frustration.

The male and female language systems differ drastically in a number of different areas. Let's take a look at some of the most basic of these: our purpose for communication, the number of words we use to communicate, the types of words we use, and the subjects we want to communicate.

Our Purpose for Communication

If I (Janis), a fairly typical wife, were to say to my husband, "Brent, we haven't talked much lately. We need to talk more," he, being a fairly typical husband, will reply, "About what?" Men and women communicate for different reasons. Men communicate in order to accomplish a task or solve a problem, while women communicate in order to build a relationship. Therefore, for men, communication must center on a certain topic, a problem that needs to be fixed, or some other information that needs to be shared. On the other hand, because women communicate for the purpose of relationship, for a woman, the topic is usually not nearly as important as the process of sharing and the drawing close that accompanies talking about the details of life. So the topic is not nearly as important to her as the act of communicating itself. In fact, she may jump from topic to topic, engaging in conversation for the purpose of feeling close to her husband. A woman is also more interested in talking about relationships. Usually, a man will only talk about relationships if he feels there is something that needs to be fixed or resolved—in other words, a task to fulfill.

Several years ago, a *Cathy* cartoon was published that illustrated this concept so well. Cathy and her boyfriend, Irving, were sitting on a couch, and in her thought bubble, there is a little heart, so we know that she is thinking about her relationship with Irving. But in Irving's thought bubble, there is a basketball, and so we know that his mind is on the sports page of the newspaper!

In the next frame, Cathy begins to frown, although Irving is still quite satisfied with his thoughts of the basketball game. In the next frame, a conversation begins:

Cathy: "We need to talk, Irving."
Irving: "We've been talking all day, Cathy."
Cathy: "But we haven't really *talked* talked."
Irving: "What do you want to talk about?"
Cathy: "I want you to talk about things."
Irving: "I'll talk about anything you want."
Cathy: "I want you to be the one to bring the subject up."
Irving: "What subject?!?"
Cathy: "Us. Irving, the only time we ever talk about us is when I bring it up. I want you to bring it up."
Irving: "What about us?"
Cathy: "I want you to bring up things between us that we need to talk about."
Irving: "What things?!?"
Cathy: "Aaaahhhh!"

Irving: "Did all that count as talking, or am I still supposed to come up with something?"[2]

Does that sound familiar? If we don't understand the basic "wiring differences" between men and women, it is easy to get frustrated with each other or think that our spouse is "broken," just doesn't do things "right," or worse, is uncaring or insensitive.

We just have to understand that men and women talk for different purposes, for different reasons. Men need to have a focus, a problem to solve, a task to accomplish, but women communicate for the purpose of building relationships.

This is what many of us see when we come home from work at the end of the day. You both arrive home and enter the same house, and immediately the wife begins to communicate for the purpose of building relationship: "Wow, did I have a rough day today! I had six back-to-back meetings and didn't get to go to lunch until two. I had lunch with Susan from accounting, and all she could talk about were the budget cuts that are coming up. I don't know how we can keep going with this much work and now maybe even fewer employees..." She is sharing what is occurring in her life in order to draw close to her husband. She doesn't need him to help her with her work situation; she just wants him to have the details of her life in order to be connected. Her husband, however, let's hypothetically call him "Brent," being a left-brained male, assumes that she is communicating for the same reason he does, to solve a problem. He immediately thinks, *Aha! I need to correct this situation. There is a task here in front of me that needs my attention!* And before the wife can even finish her "story," the husband has jumped in with a solution: "Honey! What you need to do is . . . !" And he has no idea why she shuts down, leaves the room, and slams the door behind her.

If you get nothing else out of this book, husbands, you need to know that what your wife is trying to do is to feel close to you, her man. She is saying, "I want to tell you what's going on in my life because I like you, and I want to feel close to you. . . You don't need to tell me what to do, because I don't need you to 'fix it.' I can fix it on my own. I just want you to understand." All she needs from you is a listening ear. I, let's *hypothetically* call me "Brent" again, know this is hard, because just listening doesn't feel like we are doing anything. But we have to change our perspective and know that "just listening" *is* accomplishing something. It is making our wives feel loved and supported.

And wives, I (Janis) want to share with you that usually our husbands aren't trying to "fix us" or our problems because they think we are inadequate or incapable, but from the man's perspective, he is saying, "I love you, I don't want you to be in pain, and I want to accomplish this task for you. I don't want you to experience this problem, so the best thing I can do is to make it go away for you." He is not trying to fix things because he is insensitive; it is because he doesn't want you to hurt. Many fights between couples begin because of this lack of under-standing of the different reasons why we communicate.

Interestingly, we women do the same thing when it comes to people we feel protective of and want to take care of—especially our children. I remember our oldest son several years ago coming home from school and saying, "Mom, I really had a big problem in gym class today. . . " I didn't need to hear anything else! I quit listening to any of the details, because my child had a problem and Super Mom was ready to leap into action! We don't want to see our children in pain, and our immediate response is usually, "What do I need to do about this?" I jumped right into, "Do I need to call the coach? Do I need to call the principal? What can I *do* to take care of this?" He looked at me as seriously as a fifth grader can and said, "Mom, I don't want you to do anything! *Please,* don't do anything! All I wanted to do was to let you know what was going on!"

What we all need to understand—both men who are listening to their wives, and mothers who are listening to their children—is that *sometimes just listening is enough!* And one way that wives really help their husbands is by simply letting them know "why" we are communicating: "Sweetheart, I just want to share with you some stuff that's going on, but you don't need to do anything about it. I'm just sharing because I want you to know, okay?" That kind of statement will take the pressure off of a man, so that he realizes that you don't *want* him to do anything about it; you just want him to be a part of your life.

The Number of Words We Use

One of the biggest differences in communication between men and women is the number of words that they speak. The average woman speaks about 25,000 words per day. We have had some women in our seminars comment that their husbands only speak about five words per day, based on how they communicate when they come home: "Is my dinner ready yet?" But the truth is that men actually speak about half the number of words that women do: 12,500 words, on average.[3]

We learned this truth very early on in our marriage. We'd come home about the same time each day from the office where we both worked. As soon as the door was shut, I (Brent) would say, "So how was your day, Janis?" That was all I needed to say to get her started.

Janis would follow me through the apartment sharing the details of her day: "Well, at eight o'clock, I had a meeting over in the other building. Did you know they put new carpet down in there? You wouldn't believe the color—I don't know what they were thinking, because it doesn't match the furniture or the walls AT ALL. Maybe they got, like, a thousand rolls at a really good price, but it smelled like carpet glue, and I couldn't believe they decided to have the meeting there."

All of this time, I would be changing my clothes, walking through the house, eventually settling into my chair, and once Janis had finished with every detail of her day, she would ask, "So. What did you do today, honey?"

My response, being a fairly typical male, was: "Well, I went to work and had a pretty good day." We both went to work, we both probably had the same amount of interaction with people, but whereas Janis could take twenty minutes to give me a description of her day, I could pretty well sum it up in thirty seconds! The problem was that while I knew everything that was going on in Janis's life, she knew very little of my world. I could feel close to her, because there was nothing hidden. She could only guess at what I was experiencing or feeling because I shared so little.

Needless to say, this was the cause of a lot of misunderstandings and hurt feelings. Men and women are different! We communicate differently! Of course, we can't discount the role that personality types and environmental factors play in our makeup, but it is true that women will, as a general rule, talk much more than men will. Part of this lies in where we draw our self-esteem from. Men draw the majority of their self-esteem from the tasks that they perform, from their work and their hobbies, but women draw the majority of their self-esteem from the relationships that they are cultivating, the primary one being their relationship with their husbands—and relationships require communication to thrive. I (Brent) finally came to realize that if Janis was drawing a lot of her self-esteem from her relationship with me, I wasn't giving her very much in my thirty seconds a day.

Eventually, I learned that "listening" and "talking" were both tasks that I could "perform" to help build our marriage. While I didn't just one day suddenly jump out of bed with the desire to share every little detail of my life, I did begin to say to myself, *I need to give Janis more information. I need to start telling her more of what's going on inside of me. I need to communicate with her more.* Now, I'll never be longwinded and give her every detail of my day, but I have learned to come up with things to share with her that keep her connected and involved in my life.

And I (Janis) have learned that Brent isn't withholding information to try to be distant, and he is not uncaring. He is just different than I am, and we will always communicate differently. There is value in those differences, and it's a process of making those differences work *for* us and our relationship.

The Kinds of Words We Use

Not only do men and women differ in their purpose for communication and the number of words that they use, they also use different *kinds* of words.

A Stanford University study once put microphones on preschool boys and girls in a playground to record their types and levels of communication. The results showed a marked difference in the communication of little boys and little girls, even at that young age. One hundred percent of the noises that the little girls made to each other and to their dolls were actual words and sentences; they were attempting to communicate very clearly to those around them.

On the other hand, only 68 percent of the noises coming out of the little boys' mouths were actual articulated words. The rest of the sounds were noises like, "Grrrrraaaww!" "Bang, bang, bang!" "K-k-k-k-k," or other nonsense-sounding war or fighting sounds. They were "shooting 'em up," "bang-banging the guns," or otherwise "karate chopping" their opponents with grunts, groans, and even howls. Even from that young age, it is obvious that there are some drastic differences between male and female communication![4]

The Subjects We Talk About

Studies of adult communication show that about 23 percent of the topics men discuss are actually personal or relational in nature. Everything else has to do with accomplishing a task, something to do with work, something that is not personal, emotional, or relational in any way. On the other hand, a whopping 60 percent of female conversations are made up of personal, relational topics.

Husbands, children, friends, neighbors, co-workers: These are the things that women converse about the most.[5]

We have seen this clearly when we go over to visit another couple for dinner and spend the evening. The men tend to congregate in the den or the living room, often with a sports program on TV, while the women group together in the kitchen or some other room for much of the evening. On the drive back home, as we "compare notes" on what is going on in the lives of our friends, we see a big difference in what has been communicated over the evening. Have you ever noticed the difference?

Janis will say, "So, what did you guys talk about all night?" And I will respond, "Well, the playoffs were the big topic, and Jim's business is really picking up."

When it's Janis's turn, she knows every detail of the other couples' lives. She will say something like, "I didn't know Steve and Mara were having financial problems. Did you know that they're on the verge of bankruptcy? And their oldest child, they think he might have attention deficit disorder! They just took him in to have him tested, and now they're trying to decide if they should put him on the medicine or not. And Rachel's mother might have to move in with her and Jim because she's having some real health problems, but they don't know how they're going to work it all out." We spent the same amount of time together in the same house, but while the men talked only about surface, task-oriented topics, the women were sharing details of each other's lives. The women were communicating to build relationships. The men didn't see any tasks to be solved in a social evening, so their conversation remained superficial.

It's interesting that nine out of ten speech problems occur in little boys, not little girls. Boys have much more difficulty with learning how to speak.[6] Did you know (now, men don't use this against your wife), that they have even done studies of newborn infants still in the hospital, and female babies actually have more lip movement immediately after birth than the male babies do?[7] Women are hardwired to be communicators, almost from day one, but that doesn't mean that men *can't* communicate. God made men and women different for His own purposes, and when He brings us together in relationship, we must learn how to communicate clearly with each other, in each other's language, in order to maximize our strengths and bring the best of both worlds into the relationship.

So how do we do this? How can we learn to speak each other's language? There's a lot of material out there on communication, and most of it involves some of the following guidelines or principles.

Top Ten Communication Guidelines

1. Be a ready listener, and do not answer until the other person has finished talking.
2. Be slow to speak, think first, and don't be hasty in your words; speak in such a way that the other person can understand and accept what you say.
3. Speak the truth always, but do it in love.
4. Do not use silence to frustrate the other person. Explain why you're hesitant to talk at a particular time.
5. Do not become involved in quarrels; it is possible to disagree without quarreling.
6. Do not respond in anger. Use a soft and kind response.
7. When you are in the wrong, admit it, and ask for forgiveness. When someone confesses a wrong to you, tell the person that you forgive him or her. Be sure it is forgotten, and not continually brought up in that person's presence.
8. Avoid nagging.
9. Do not blame or criticize the other person, but restore him, encourage him, and edify him. If someone verbally attacks, criticizes, or blames you, do not respond in the same manner.
10. Try to understand the other person's opinion. Make allowances for any differences. Be concerned about his or her interests.

What a wonderful list of guidelines! Wouldn't life be great if we could all follow all of them, all of the time! Easier said than done. We don't live in a perfect world, and unfortunately, most of us are affected by what we like to call the "Sunday Sermon/ Monday Morning Syndrome."

We all know what it's like to sit in a church service and get all fired up by the pastor's message. You know, you suddenly decide you are going to start getting up at 5 a.m. every morning to pray and read the Bible; you're going to start exercising; you're going to have family devotions, be kinder to your spouse, get to know your neighbors; the list could go on and on. But come Monday morning, the "high" of the sermon has worn off, and when the alarm clock goes off at 7:15, all thoughts of prayer and Bible study have vanished from your mind. Your biggest concern is fighting the traffic and getting in to the office on time. Before you know it, Tuesday, Wednesday, and Thursday have passed, and you haven't gone to the gym, you've snapped at your spouse every day, and the thought of family devotions is a distant memory. Can you relate?

The same thing happens with the "Top Ten Communication Guidelines." Most of us would agree that putting them into practice would be a tremendous help to our marriages, and our lives in general, but for many, it just never materializes in real life. What can we do to change this? How can we begin to understand the other person's language system and start *really* communicating with our mate?

What Filter Are You Using?

About six months into our marriage, we bought our first car. We were so proud of it, and even though the payments weren't that high by today's standards, they were sure high enough for us. We had determined our budget, and we knew that we could afford it—as long as nothing drastic changed in our financial situation.

Everything was going well, until one day Janis had a bad day at work, and she came home and told me about it: "I hate my job!" she cried. "I should *not* have to put up with the stuff I'm putting up with. I am *so* out of there! There is no way I'm going to work under those conditions another day! I am so angry at how they are treating me there!" And on and on she went about the situation that had taken place and prompted her anger.

I listened . . . for about thirty seconds until I heard the words, "I am so out of there!" As soon as I realized she was talking about quitting her job, my mind shut down at that point in the conversation and would go no further. All I could think about was the car payments we needed to make, how we would miss one, and then another, and soon the bank would repossess the beautiful new car we were so proud of.

Meanwhile, Janis had continued in the conversation, and was sharing how angry she was about what had happened to her. But I saw a problem that *desperately* needed to be fixed! And so I jumped in: "Honey, it's going to be okay," I blurted out, completely cutting her off. "This is what you need to do. Tomorrow morning, you need to go and talk to your supervisor and tell him exactly what's going on. If that doesn't work, you can go back to your desk and write a memo to *his* supervisor. . ."

To me, it was a brilliant plan. It fixed Janis's problem, allowed her to keep her job, and allowed us both to keep the new car! What could be wrong with that?

Unfortunately, in the middle of my "fix-it speech," I barely noticed that Janis's eyes were filling with tears, which very soon began to drip down her cheeks. By the time I was finished, she was sobbing, and then she blurted out, "You are so cold and insensitive! You could care less about how I'm feeling! You are more concerned about that precious new car and my paycheck than you are about me!"

What was merely an effort made by Janis to share her bad day with me turned into a very ugly, very long argument. In fact, as we recall it, it lasted three hours and went from room to room in our apartment, each of us saying all kinds of ugly things to each other and about each other and even about each other's heritage! The ironic thing was that afterward, we realized we didn't even disagree about the situation. At the end of it all, I realized that Janis didn't actually intend to quit her job—she was just venting, emphasizing how bad her day had been.

And I (Janis) realized that Brent *did*, in fact, care about me. He didn't want me to stay in a job that I hated—he wanted me to be happy.

Because we were both halfway through our graduate degrees in marriage and family counseling, we thought that if we wanted to stay married, or help anyone else stay married, we'd better figure out what in the world was going wrong.

We realized that the problem was that we all have various filters through which we view the world and through which we communicate to other people. These filters correspond with the three basic aspects of the soul of man: the mind, the will, and the emotions. The filter related to the mind is our thoughts; the filter related to the will is our wants and desires; and the filter related to the emotions is our feelings. Each one of us has different thoughts, feelings, and wants, and we tend to communicate through these filters. All is well until we attempt communication with someone who is operating in a completely different filter—like the person that we married! We have to become aware of these in our own lives and then learn to share them with our spouse. So what exactly are these filters? Here are some easy definitions of each.

Thought: *An interpretation of an event; a left-brained function; a logical, rational process of our lives.*

It's important to realize that *thoughts are not facts; they are only opinions.* Just because we may think something is true, that does not necessarily make it true. Our thoughts are how we see the world. They are the result of our interpreting life through our upbringing and life experiences.

Feeling: *A spontaneous emotional response. It's spontaneous, in that it happens instantly; it's emotional, in that it involves the right-brain function of the emotions; and it's a response, in that it is a reaction to a situation or circumstance in our lives.*

It's important to realize that the feelings that we have are usually *involuntary,* and they are a *reality*. If someone were to take a sledgehammer and bring it down on your big toe, it would hurt. You would *feel* pain—even if that person were to apologize profusely for having injured you. The pain is still real, no matter how much you wish it wasn't, or how unintentionally it was inflicted. Feelings are part of our reality; we can't just wish them away. If you've been hurt, or if you have hurt someone else, that hurt doesn't just magically disappear once an apology has been given. It takes time and a healing process for feelings to be mended.

I (Brent) spent a lot of time early in our marriage trying to talk Janis out of her feelings. If I didn't do something to intentionally hurt her, I thought that she should not be hurt. We are not saying that feelings are ultimate truth. If they were, then we should make all of our decisions out of our feelings, which would lead to a pretty chaotic life. What we are saying is that they are a person's reality and are just as important as the other two areas of awareness.

Want: *A desire; something we want to see happen; something we want to possess.*

This can become confusing because sometimes our wants are in conflict with each other. We have all experienced this in our financial world. I want to pay off debt or build a big college fund for my children, but I also want to buy that brand-new car! These are conflicting wants within ourselves. That's when clear communication is imperative in order to avoid issues. We have a responsibility to communicate our wants to our partners—not just the obvious desires, or the desires that "sound good," but all of our wants, because it is generally those unspoken wants and desires we have that will cause the most trouble in a relationship.

This is what happens when you have just attended a financial seminar together and decided to cut back and accumulate savings, and then one of you makes what we call a "mall run" or surprises the other with a new bass boat! While we may look irrational (and our spouse may even call us "crazy"), it is actually because we didn't express our hidden wants. We only expressed the ones that seemed socially acceptable in the context of the financial seminar.

Most of the time, husbands and wives are speaking to each other out of different filters. If we go back to our earlier example, when Janis was trying to communicate how bad her day actually was, she was approaching the conversation through a "feeling filter," but I (Brent) was receiving her words through the "thought filter." She was conveying a *feeling* by saying how bad her day was and a *want* that she wanted to quit her job; I perceived that as a *thought,* a logical recourse that she was about to take. And because of this miscommunication, an argument was the result. After our three hours of misery, we discovered that we both had the same thoughts about her need to leave her job in the right timing and the right way so that we wouldn't lose our car. And I (Janis) realized that Brent did feel

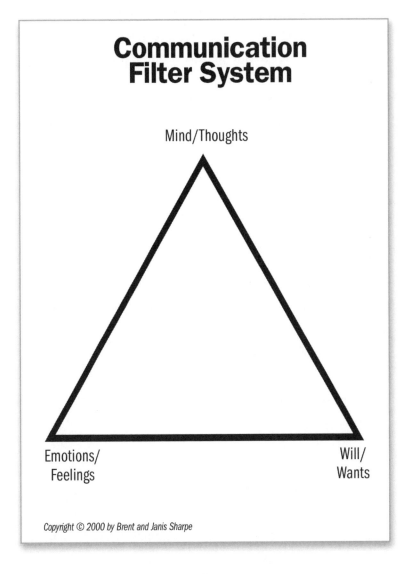

Communication Filter System

Mind/Thoughts

Emotions/
Feelings

Will/
Wants

Copyright © 2000 by Brent and Janis Sharpe

bad that I was miserable in my job, and he wasn't being insensitive. We were just hearing different parts of the same situation and totally misunderstanding each other.

Reaching Mutual Understanding

Think about the last time you were in a classroom setting. Let's say that you are in a class, and you had just had a test the day before. When the professor came in to start the lecture, you knew that the information he was about to give would not be tested on for at least three or four more weeks. How likely is it that you will pay close attention in class?

Now, consider how you would pay attention if the professor came in and said, "Today we will have a pop quiz at the end of this class period!" Your listening skills would probably greatly improve! Because we know that we will have to repeat the information that we just heard, the most important priority becomes listening.

Avoiding communication mishaps with your partner, learning to *really* listen to what he or she has to say, will require just this sort of active listening. This can be practiced through an exercise we call "Mutual Understanding."

Mutual Understanding is like taking a little test on what your partner has just said. When your partner finishes speaking, the idea is to repeat back what you've heard, not by parroting the words exactly, but *in your own words*. This allows the person who started the conversation to hear how the message was received and then confirm or clarify the information. It may be awkward at first, but it is an effective tool to learning to listen actively, to look for the meaning behind the filters, to really hear what your partner is saying. Take a look at what the conversation about Janis's bad day might have been like if Mutual Understanding (see diagram on page 125) had been practiced.

Janis: "I hate my job! I should *not* have to put up with the stuff I'm putting up with. I am *so* out of there! There is no way I'm going to work under those conditions another day! I am so angry at how they are treating me there!"

Brent: [After having heard her out, and realizing I am having a reaction to what is being said, I take a moment to make sure that I have heard her accurately before letting myself react to what I think she is saying. I would repeat back to her what I think she said.] "Honey, it sounds like you have had a really bad day. I am really sorry it was so rough. It sounds like it was bad enough that you wanted to quit. Did you quit?"

Janis: [This gives me an opportunity to clarify what I said to help him understand the true meaning.] "I wish! No, I know I can't do that."

Brent: [If that is not enough information, we may need to repeat again our understanding to further clarify.] "But I heard you say that today was really bad. Are you thinking about quitting?"

Janis: "I'd love to quit, and I want to, but I know that we have the car payments we have to make. I just can't stay there much longer. I guess I may need to try to find another job."

At this point, I (Brent) would be able to relax and continue to listen for the emotion in Janis's words, rather than begin to panic with thoughts of losing our car.

Brent: "I really want you to be happy. Tell me more about what has frustrated you about your day."

Just clarifying what I heard and getting information that I understood would have eliminated all the misery that we went through.

But I (Janis) could have also taken the responsibility to let Brent know that I was sharing feelings and that my intentions were not to walk out of my job. A simple statement such as, "Boy, do I need to vent about my day!" would have lowered Brent's blood pressure and been clearer communication.

Good communication will significantly reduce issues but not eradicate them completely. Unfortunately, there are those situations in which Janis could have come in the house, shared the same information, and then blurted out, "I quit my job today!" We would have had good communication, but we definitely would have had a problem because I (Brent) would have not agreed with that decision! Good communication skills can help to diffuse many issues that aren't really issues but were just misunderstandings, but it won't prevent them altogether. Some conflict is inevitable, because we are different—men and women, in our personalities, and in our upbringings. We will view life differently, and inevitably issues will arise. Good communication will help make sure that we are not experiencing conflict over things about which we don't really disagree.

Conflict in a marriage is a reality, and in itself, isn't bad, but it's how we handle conflict that matters. The next chapter will help you learn to not be afraid of conflict, how to face issues when they arise, and how to end up with a stronger marriage as a result.

Team Building Exercise 6

Take a few minutes to sit down with your spouse and each of you think of a topic to discuss. Each of you should have your own. Pick a topic that is not a personal one; this is to insure that this could not possibly turn into a real conflict between the two of you. It could be how your day went or about something you read in the newspaper, but make sure it has some detail to it, not just where you want to go for lunch. After you have chosen your topic, begin the exercise by one of you sharing your topic. Your partner draws the triangle we discussed on a piece of paper with the three parts labeled: thoughts, feelings, and wants. As the first partner tells his story, the other is listening for the parts and writing a few words that will help her remember what was said, such as: thoughts in the thought section, feelings separated out, and so on. So, while one spouse is talking, the other is only listening and writing. Once the first partner is finished, the second tries to tell the first what she heard: "These were the thoughts I heard," etc. The first listens to see if what was heard was accurate and confirms or clarifies until both feel that they have the same understanding. Once this is done, reverse the roles so that both people have the chance to be the sender and the receiver.

Team Building Exercise 7

Take 21 days and practice repeating back what your partner says as he or she shares about important things in his or her life. Don't wait until you have an emotional reaction to do this. If you practice on things that are important but that don't create negative emotion, it will be easier to do it later with more emotionally charged issues. Go overboard a little, and have fun with it for three weeks to help form the habit of listening in a way that you can repeat back what your partner is saying. If you listen this way, you will begin to hear the heart of your partner and be able to accurately interpret his or her meaning.

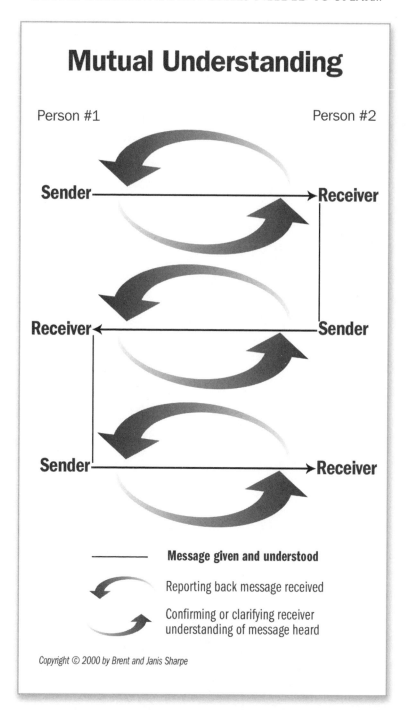

CHAPTER 7

ISSUE RESOLUTION: RESOLVING ISSUES IN A WAY THAT BUILDS INTIMACY

In a successful marriage, there is no such thing as one's way. There is only the way of both, only the bumpy, dusty, difficult, but always mutual path.
—Phyllis McGinley

I N OUR WORK WITH COUPLES over the past twenty years, if there was one thing that we have seen as a theme of unsatisfying marriages, it is the inability of couples to deal with issues in their relationship in a productive way. As a matter of fact, from our perspective, the number-one reason for a lack of emotional intimacy is unresolved issues or conflict. God's plan was that two unique and different people would blend and mold their lives into one, which would allow for greater strength as a team. The challenge is that in our culture we have not learned effective "blending and molding" procedures, so when we draw toward each other, we begin to bump into things that we don't agree on, and tension and frustration begin. Because we don't handle these tensions very well, we end up pulling back from one another to just keep the peace, because no one wants to feel upset all the time. We learn what not to bring up and what not to talk about, and so we begin to limit the areas of life we can even discuss, ending up with what we call a "roommate marriage." We may be able to sit in the stands of our child's ball game, visit with neighbors together, handle a car purchase, or other functions of life, but we experience no real emotional intimacy and quickly become dissatisfied. So one of the most critical skills in marriage is dealing with differences and blending the unique gifts we both bring to the table in a way that creates strength.

Every relationship has issues that create conflict—because every relationship consists of two or more people who are different from each other and whose differences will eventually come to the surface. Issues come from two different sources.

The first type of issue surfaces when two people are communicating, and they suddenly realize that they have a disagreement. Because the communication is good, they each can clearly see that one of them thinks or feels one way on the subject, and the other thinks or feels very differently. The question then becomes, who is right? Who will "win" in this situation? Of course, our challenge as humans is that we all believe our way is the right way. We may think, *If you agree with me, then you are very bright, and I really like you. If you don't agree with me, then because I know I am right and you disagree with me, you must be wrong, and I need to convince you of my "rightness" and your "wrongness."* Thus the battle is on. Research tells us that in only 30 percent of discussions over disagreements, one partner will ever come to agree that the other is right—which leaves 70 percent of disagreements unresolvable unless the couple has developed an effective issue-resolution strategy.[1]

The second type of issue is a little more difficult to pin down. It includes those little and big things that your partner does or doesn't do that really irritate you, offend you, or drive you crazy. You know what we are talking about! You want to overlook them or even try to ignore them, but they just keep on frustrating or hurting you. The other person may not even be aware of the conflict he or she has caused; but the issue is there nonetheless.

So issues can be overt—out there in plain sight for all to see—or they may be covert, with only one person even aware that an issue exists. Regardless of which type of issue comes up in your relationship, it needs to be resolved for there to be honest, open interaction between you and your spouse and for you to have a warm and intimate relationship.

There are four primary patterns into which all of us fall when we are trying to resolve these issues or conflicts. Most people will actually fall into one of the first three of these patterns, and the reason for that is that in our society, we are indoctrinated with the need to win.

Unfortunately, most of the time, for one person to win, another person must lose. And when this principle is practiced in a marriage, the results are often disastrous. By encouraging a win-lose culture in our marriages, we are perpetuating the fact that someone will continually be losing—and conflicts will never be truly resolved. When one person or the other is losing, one or the other will always be dissatisfied, so that you are either happy and content in your marriage, or you are frustrated and dissatisfied, all depending on whether or not you have "won" the latest round of conflict. Can you see how this would set up a competitive spirit within a marriage? If I'm going to be happy and content, I must win, and for me to win, you must lose. And the issues that are never really resolved—the ones that are simply "won" or "lost"—become those issues that are carried around by the "loser," sometimes for years. Needless to say, this is not an environment in which a happy, healthy marriage will flourish.

Patterns of Resolving Conflict

Of the four different patterns of resolving conflict, the first three are negative patterns that most people fall into when they are confronted by conflict: passive, aggressive, and passive-aggressive.

The Passive Pattern. Do you remember on the show *All in the Family*, Archie and Edith Bunker had all kinds of conflict all of the time? But because Edith was a classic passive personality, their issues were never actually resolved. She put up with everything that Archie dished out, so that he always ended up getting his own way, and he became a real challenge to live with!

Most passive people:

- Don't honestly say what they think or feel.
- Allow others to choose for them.
- Do not achieve their own goals.
- Have a tendency to give up easily in conflict.
- Are constantly taken advantage of.

- ❧ Allow their needs to be considered as less important in a relationship.
- ❧ Are filled with insecurity.
- ❧ Feel like a victim.
- ❧ Are often frustrated and unhappy.
- ❧ Are unwilling to take responsibility for their own behavior.
- ❧ Take too much responsibility for the behavior of others.
- ❧ Try to make other people happy.
- ❧ Eagerly desire to "keep the peace."

When a conflict or an issue arises, passive people tend to "stuff" their emotional reaction deep inside, choosing instead to pretend that everything is okay. They put a lid on their feelings and hold it in, rather than be emotionally honest with their partner about what is going on inside of them. But what many passive people fail to realize is that this emotional pressure that they are stuffing deep inside will come out eventually, one way or another. For many people, it shows up as a physical illness, or they may begin to experience emotional extremes—one day they may be completely happy, but the next day they may be completely depressed—all because of the emotional draining that is taking place from their "stuffed" feelings.

Perhaps one of the most devastating consequences that can be derived from a passive personality is that of becoming a *pleaser*.[2] A pleaser personality is formed when a passive personality is allowed to run amok. It is passivity to an extreme. The pleaser says, "I will completely change my desires in order to make you happy. What I want doesn't really matter anyway; it is all about what you want and need." Pleasers don't attend to their own needs and wants. They refuse to be honest, because, to them, keeping the peace is more important than an honest, open relationship. Pleasers will tend to lose in conflict, and they will often feel like a victim. In reality, this is their attempt to get their own needs met. Pleasers believe if they can make their partner happy, then their partner will be in a good mood and treat them right—and the pleaser will ultimately be happy. Unfortunately, it does not work. Eventually, if they continue in this line of behavior, they may even lose track of their own personality, cheating themselves, their partners, and the world of who God created them to be.

The Aggressive Pattern. In the show *All in the Family*, while Edith was the passive partner in the marriage, Archie was definitely the aggressive one! He didn't hesitate to tell anyone who would listen what he was thinking or feeling—nor did he balk at sharing what he thought *others* should be thinking or feeling, as well. While the passive person swallows his or her emotions and stuffs them deep inside, the aggressive person does just the opposite, spitting out anything that comes to mind, regardless of what the consequences are for him or anyone else around him. For the aggressive person, life is a series of explosions.

Most aggressive people:

- Tell you what you ought to think or feel.
- Make decisions for other people.
- Achieve their goals at the expense of others.
- Violate other people's needs to get their own needs met.
- Appear to be confident, but in actuality, are very insecure.
- Have negative self-esteem.
- Frequently blame other people for their problems.

- ✂ Will do whatever it takes to "win."
- ✂ Are very controlling of other people, especially their mates.

Aggressive personalities will do whatever it takes to "win" in the marriage; they will lie, cheat, or even appear to be honest, if that is what it takes to achieve their goals. They will win at all costs.

Frequently, an aggressive person will attract a passive personality, and many marriages are made up of an aggressive person who has married a passive person. These two personality types will attract each other like magnets, and while they usually fit together fairly well (there is little conflict because the aggressor always wins and the passive person always acquiesces), it is not a healthy marriage. Unless a conflict is resolved with a win-win solution, everybody loses. Even if the aggressive personality is constantly "winning," the arguments in a marriage, he or she is not really winning, because the marriage itself is losing out.

The Passive-Aggressive Pattern. Rather than Edith or Archie in *All in the Family*, the television character who best portrays the passive-aggressive pattern is the spinach-eating Popeye. Do you remember how he would react to the conflicts that came his way? Bluto, the strong, muscular sailor, would always beat up on Popeye, and Popeye would just put up with it, for almost the entire cartoon. But then there would come a point at which Popeye would get fed up, and then would come the famous words: "I've hads enuf! I can't stands no more!" Out popped the spinach, Popeye sucked it down his pipe, and immediately his biceps began to bulge! Whenever Popeye finally got angry, he *really* got angry, and everybody knew it.

Popeye's reaction is the classic passive-aggressive pattern that characterizes many people. They stuff their anger and ignore their frustration until finally something happens that becomes the "straw that broke the camel's back." They hold it in, and hold it in, and then suddenly, out of nowhere, it seems, they blow up in anger. Only it isn't just "out of nowhere"—their anger has been building in them for hours, days, weeks, even years, until finally they "can't stands no more!"

It may have happened in your house. The husband comes home from work, shuts the door behind him, and then throws his coat down on the couch. And the wife goes through the ceiling: "You never help out around here! Why do I always have to clean up after you? You are such a slob!"

The issue isn't just the one time that her husband threw the coat on the couch. Chances are, she's been holding some things in for a while, and the coat was just the last straw that set off her anger.

Passive-aggressive patterns can be confusing to other people who are unaware that there are any underlying problems. The husband may have been completely clueless that he had been doing anything at all that bothered his wife—until she blew! And chances are, because he suddenly felt himself being attacked, he is likely to react to her in an aggressive manner—and a full-fledged fight is underway.

Another expression of a passive-aggressive pattern is an underground style. These personalities don't actually blow up outwardly; they just get quiet and sarcastic and build internal resentments. They may make quiet cutting comments, but when confronted, will say they were only teasing, or they didn't really mean it the way it was taken. Sometimes their resentments come out in nonverbal ways, such as overspending or overeating, in order to get back at their spouse.

These three patterns—passive, aggressive, and passive-aggressive—are the three responses to conflict that most people naturally take. And without God's help and intervention, these are frequently the only three ways in which we are likely to respond. Unfortunately, all three of these patterns bring about a "win-lose" situation.

The only option in a healthy marriage is "win-win." So how can we bring about "win-win" solutions in our marriages? There is a fourth possible response to conflict—one that is biblical and healthy. That is the *assertive pattern*.

The Assertive Pattern. When we respond assertively to our differences in marriage, we can create "win-win" solutions from our conflicts. In our culture, people frequently equate the terms *aggressive* and *assertive*. But for our purposes in this book, they are vastly different.

Rather than swallowing how they feel or, at the other extreme, demanding that others feel or act a certain way, assertive people clearly state how they themselves feel. Assertive people are interested in how the other person feels, but they don't hide their own ideas or emotions; instead, they work to find a solution that meets the needs of everyone involved.

Most assertive people:

- Take ownership of their thoughts and emotions.
- Share equally and openly, without being controlling.
- Choose for themselves, rather than choosing for others, or allowing others to choose for them.
- Achieve their goals, without taking advantage of others.

- ❧ Respect the needs of both others and themselves.
- ❧ Are secure in themselves.
- ❧ Take responsibility for their own lives.
- ❧ Are uncritically honest and straightforward.
- ❧ Negotiate for reasonable change.

An assertive person is someone who feels good about himself and about the other person, someone who says, "I count and you count too. We're both important in this situation; let's come to some kind of agreement that we can both live with, that can be positive for both of us." They realize that the best solution will be one in which they have worked together and negotiated to come up with the best possible solution for everyone involved.

Now, it is easy for us to agree that assertive behavior is the best behavior to follow—but putting it into practice in real life is a lot more challenging! Most of us already have our set patterns of attempting to deal with conflict—and they fall into the passive, aggressive, or passive-aggressive categories. It's a dance we do with our partners—and we know the steps well.

Let's say Sally gets mad, so she goes into the kitchen and slams the door. When her husband, Josh, doesn't respond and instead walks over to his recliner, leans back, and shuts his eyes, she starts to slam a few cabinet doors. She will continue doing any attention-getting behavior that she normally does to alert him that there is a problem. And he probably will use whatever his normal habits are to avoid acknowledging the problem. Eventually, she will walk into the living room and stand in front of him until he opens one eye and says, "What's the matter with you?"

Her response? "Well, if you don't know by now, I'm not going to tell you!"

He usually has a set response to that statement—and so on it goes. The issues may change, but the "dance" never does. Can you relate?

The reason this happens is because each of us has brought into the marriage emotional bruises that are soft spots in our hearts. If our partner does something that hurts us or doesn't do something that is important to us, and it hits our soft spot, we have an emotional reaction. We react out of our emotions, and we do something in retaliation. Unfortunately, this usually hits our partner's own soft spot, and he or she reacts, as well, which usually hits our soft spot again, causing our same emotional reaction and retaliation—and on and on it goes. We get caught in this "dance," and usually it escalates until someone finally gets fed up and shuts down or walks out. The whole situation is so painful and frustrating that we eventually learn that it's better to not bring it up again. We just avoid that issue from then on and find ourselves slowly pulling away and distancing ourselves from our partner. Our emotional intimacy quickly dries up.

Many years ago, Janis and I found out we had our own dance in our marriage. We found ourselves both feeling and doing the same thing in our discussions no matter what topic we were struggling with. I (Brent) discovered my soft spot is that I felt like a failure in our marriage and thought I wouldn't be able to properly learn Janis's language and meet her needs. When something happened and I started to feel like I had blown it again, my reaction was to get quiet and pull back emotionally. I would justify and rationalize my behavior and try to explain to her why she shouldn't feel the way she did because I didn't mean to hurt her.

Janis's soft spot was that she didn't feel special and that she felt pretty low on my priority list. When she felt that way, she would tend to say that I didn't care about her or that it didn't seem like I really loved her. Those statements hit to the heart of my own soft spot! I felt even more like a failure, and without thinking, I would pull back or try to rationalize my behavior. That made her feel *more* devalued because I was discounting her feelings, which made her say something else about how I would never understand or really care for her.

You can see how the dance can go on and on and on. But we knew that there had to be a solution. I loved Janis deeply, and she was the priority in my life. She actually never considered me a failure in our relationship or incapable of meeting her needs. But our own wounds tripped up the whole communication process and kept us from finding the solution. The ultimate answer was that we needed to sit down and talk about each issue we encountered in a way that would lead us to a win-win solution, but we had trouble breaking out of our dance to have a productive discussion. Finally, we were able to recognize the dance and realize that if we could both be aware of what we were feeling, that our reactions were out of our own hurts from the past, and if we could learn a different reaction than our natural one, we could change this unhealthy pattern into a productive one. Eventually we found that once we realized what was happening, it didn't take a lot to break the pattern. Sometimes each of us simply stating how we felt at the moment—that we didn't want to react the old way—was enough to start us down a new path.

The challenge then became, when we stopped the old unproductive dance, how could two people that have totally different viewpoints come together and walk away with a win-win solution? Fortunately, we have come up with a three-step model that can help you step out of your usual dance pattern and into the assertive pattern of resolving issues. You have a choice to change the dance! Even if your partner doesn't want to change, if you refuse to play into the old habits and patterns that you are both accustomed to, it will create a change in the relationship. As they say, "It takes two to tango!" But it only takes one person to break an unhealthy pattern in a relationship, and while you can't control what your partner will do or how he or she will react, you do have control over your own reactions, which can change the entire system.

The Top Ten Issue-Resolution Guidelines

The three-step model we are going to share with you is based on certain basic guidelines and principles that you need to understand before you begin to implement the model. We like to call these the "top ten issue-resolution guidelines." As you begin to follow these guidelines, you will begin to respond to conflict in an assertive way, rather than a passive or an aggressive way.

1. The discussion should be held in order to reach a solution, not to gain a victory.

"Be completely humble and gentle; be patient, bearing with one another in love. Make every effort to keep the unity of the Spirit through the bond of peace." —Ephesians 4:2-3

Most of us want to win. We want our own way. Because we are human, most of us are okay with a "win-lose" situation—as long as *we* are the ones on the winning side of the equation! But think of it this way: If you win an argument over your mate, you have actually lost, because your spouse is a part of you. You cannot separate yourself from your spouse, and if your mate loses, you do too. The Bible often compares unity to the parts of a physical human body that work together. Marriage can be compared to this, as well. If you were to slam your hand in the car door, the nerves in your hand would be sending messages of "Pain!" "Send help!" "Emergency!" up your arm and to your brain cells. Your hand would be saying, "Bring that other hand over here and apply some pressure where it hurts!" If the brain says, "You know, that hand isn't really important to me. It's actually insignificant to me and all of the things I am doing," where would the body be? It wouldn't function well at all, especially in a task that required two hands. But our bodies don't work like that. When one part of our body hurts, the rest of our body responds—just the way things should happen in a marriage.

The only way there can be true cohesiveness, unity, and power in a relationship is when both partners' perspectives are equally valued. The commitment must be, "We're going to solve this problem together," not, "I'm going to win!"

2. Discuss one issue at a time.

"But everything should be done in a fitting and orderly way." —1 Corinthians 14:40

The most important thing to remember at this point is to *deal with only one problem at a time!* Many times, when our partners bring up an issue about us, we get defensive and throw back another issue at them to even the score, and they may even react to that with another one of their own to offset ours. The end result is a mixing of all kinds of other issues into the original problem. Your partner may ask you to do the dishes, and you may feel hurt or believe that your spouse is thinking that you aren't carrying your load around the house. Rather than dealing with either the dishes or the underlying emotional response, you may respond, "Well, I'll do the dishes when you wash the car!" And she responds, "Well, I'll clean the car when you clean out the hallway closet!" Suddenly, there are three or four issues that have come up instead of the one that needed focus to begin with. This leads to escalation, and eventually the conversation just stops because everyone is frustrated. It is impossible to solve more than one issue at a time.

3. You cannot refuse a discussion.

"Be devoted to one another in brotherly love. Honor one another above yourselves. —Romans 12:10

If something is important to one of you, it must be considered significant and a legitimate concern that should be discussed. On the other hand, this does not mean that all of a sudden, if you think of an issue at 3 o'clock in the morning, you can wake up your partner right then and demand that a discussion take place immediately. It is preferable in that situation to set a time for a discussion, but the rule we suggest is that the discussion *must take place within 24 hours of being brought up.* In other words, one partner cannot keep delaying and delaying a discussion; and they cannot say, "That's not important; we're not going to talk about it." You cannot refuse a discussion.

4. If the discussion is a question of fact, then it's your duty to get the facts. However, if the discussion is a matter of opinion, you must recognize it as such and realize that a compromise is the only solution.

"Then you will know the truth and the truth will set you free." —John 8:32

"If you have any encouragement from being united with Christ, if any comfort from his love, if any fellowship with the Spirit, if any tenderness and compassion, then make

my joy complete by being like-minded, having the same love, being one in spirit and purpose. Do nothing out of selfish ambition or vain conceit, but in humility consider others better than yourselves. Each of you should look not only to your own interests, but also to the interests of others." —Phillipians 2:1-4

Many of the things we consider to be "facts" are, in fact, only opinions. Some things can be verified as facts; however, if there is a conflict over how much the sofa cost, that "fact" can be verified by locating the receipt or by calling the store where it was purchased. But if you are having a conflict over an opinion (such as, was the sofa "too expensive"?), you need to recognize it as such and realize that your partner's opinion is just as valid as your own. The reality is that very few times do we argue over fact; almost all conflicts deal with our perceptions and thoughts, which are merely our opinions, as much as we would like to think they are facts.

5. Don't try to mind read.

"For who among men knows the thoughts of a man except the man's spirit within him?" —1 Corinthians 2:11

It is impossible to read the mind of another person! Don't even try! Nor should you try to play psychologist with the things your partner says. Don't analyze why they say the things they say. And above all else, don't assume!

Most couples carry a lot of assumptions in their relationships. They *assume* that because he or she said *this*, he or she meant *that*. And they operate in a reactionary mode that is based on assumptions that may not even be true.

6. Don't play archaeologist.

"Get rid of all bitterness, rage and anger, brawling and slander, along with every form of malice. Be kind and compassionate to one another, forgiving each other, just as in Christ God forgave you." —Ephesians 4:31-32

In other words, don't dig things up from the past! We must learn to let go of things that have happened and been dealt with already. It is not fair to keep rehashing old history just for power or to "pad" our own argument. You may ask, "What if they did something again today that they've done for the last five years?" If something happened today that has never been fully resolved, and it is still continuing, then it is not in the past and it needs to be dealt with effectively in an assertive, healthy way.

7. No name-calling!

"With the tongue we praise our Lord and Father, and with it we curse men, who have been made in God's like-ness. Out of the same mouth come praise and cursing. My brothers, this should not be." —James 3:9-10

Obviously, you are not supposed to use profanity or otherwise call your partner demeaning or ugly names in this process. But this does not just refer to what we would consider to be "bad names." This also refers to phrases such as, "You're just like your mother!" Or, "You do that because you're a melancholy, not a sanguine like me." Or, "If you were really a man of God...." Or, "If you were the submissive wife that God wants you to be...." These kinds of statements are name-calling, as well, and they are not healthy.

8. No emotional blackmail.

> *"Do not repay evil with evil or insult with insult, but with blessing, because to this you were called so that you may inherit a blessing. For, whoever would love life and see good days must keep his tongue from evil and his lips from deceitful speech.* —1 Peter 3:9-10

This point is carried over from the last guideline. Many of the statements we make that are designed to degrade or depreciate our partners qualify as emotional blackmail. Even statements like, "If you really cared about me...," or, "If you loved God, we wouldn't be having this problem," are emotional blackmail. These kinds of statements are counterproductive, and are off-limits in an "assertive" discussion.

9. State your perspective and your opinions with observational "I" statements, rather than judgmental "you" statements.

> *"Therefore let us stop passing judgment on one another. Instead, make up your mind not to put any stumbling block, or obstacle in your brother's way."* —Romans 14:13

> *"Brothers, if someone is caught in a sin, you who are spiritual should restore him gently. But watch yourself, or you also may be tempted."* —Galatians 6:1

> *Do not judge, or you too will be judged."* —Matthew 7:1

This is probably one of the most productive, issue-resolving lessons we can learn. There is a big difference between saying, "*You* did this," and "*You* did that," and "*Your* attitude stinks!" and saying, "When this happened, I felt this way," or, "My perspective on what happened is this." "You" statements are more than likely to be perceived as attacking, and will put the other person on the defensive, frequently backing them into a corner and leading to a counterproductive argument. The word *you* always carries an emotional punch. Practice taking the sting out of your words with "I" statements instead.

10. Never interrupt.

"He who answers before listening—that is his folly and shame." —Proverbs 18:13

Each person should have the right to go ahead and say what he or she needs to say without interruption. This includes both physical interruption, in which the other person literally jumps in and cuts off what the other partner is saying, and *mental* interruptions, in which the one who is listening goes off on a mental tangent and doesn't hear a word of what the other is saying. Each person's opinion is valuable and important to be heard for effective resolution.

If these guidelines fit your value system, you don't need to worry that you have to memorize them and then struggle not to break any of them. If you learn the three-step model in the next section, you will be applying each and every one of these ten guidelines in a healthy way.

The Three-Step Model

With these guidelines in mind, you can then move into a discussion with your partner about the issue at hand. You can do this using the following three-step model summarized on page 156. Over the years, we have seen this one tool produce amazing results. Even the most conflicted couples, when dedicated to following this strategy, have been able to find the power of team-work and build closeness once again in their marriage.

Step One: Setting It Up. In this, the first step, the person who is having the problem or issue approaches the other person and asks for a time to talk. This isn't what we usually do; most of the time, when we are upset about something, we do one of two things. The first is, we want to talk about it *now*—either in person or on our cell phone. The issue comes up, and we are ready to attack. When we take that approach, however, what we are really saying is, "You don't count. I don't care what you are doing right now—it's not half as important as what I want to talk about!" That kind of attitude sets us up for failure before the discussion has even begun. But the other extreme also causes us problems—when the person who is hurt doesn't say or do anything and lets bitterness and resentment fester and grow.

Instead, by approaching your partner in gentleness and respect and asking for a convenient time to discuss the issue, you are saying, in effect, "I have a need to talk about something that is affecting me, and I value you. I honor your perspective. Your time, commitments, and schedule are as important as mine, and I see your life and opinions as being as significant as my own."

The basic guideline we recommend to convey this message is asking for a specific time to talk. We recommend that you both agree that if one asks to talk, you need to set a time within twenty-four hours. You can change this timeframe to suit your particular needs, but we have found that twenty-four hours is more than enough time—but not too much—to give both part-ners a chance to set other things aside and really focus on the issue at hand.

In other words, if your spouse comes to you and says, "Honey, I really need to talk about something with you. When would be a good time?" you cannot just say, "Well, I don't want to talk right now; how about Christmas Day ten years from now?" A reasonable timeframe should be followed.

The partner who is being approached should be the one to determine when the discussion should take place. In other words, if you approach your spouse about an issue, and in your mind, it appears that she is not doing anything important, you *still* can't demand that she discuss the issue at that very moment. Part of treating the other person with respect is allowing him or her the chance to regroup and schedule a time that works best for him or her. After all, you have had plenty of time to think things over before you brought up the issue—it's respectful and honoring to offer your partner twenty-four hours! We draw this step from Ephesians 4:26, which states, "'In your anger do not sin': Do not let the sun go down while you are still angry, and do not give the devil a foothold." In our experience, we have seen this scripture taken too literally at times, and people can get into a midnight conversation that they shouldn't be having because they are too tired at that time. We don't think this scripture passage means that we have to hurry up and solve everything before the sun goes down—it just means that we shouldn't let things pile up. Deal with things as they arise to keep issues from stealing the life from your marriage. Certainly, if your partner presents an issue, you should try to talk as soon as possible, but you do have the option of setting another time within the twenty-four-hour period.

Step Two: Sharing the Problem. When you sit down to share the problem, the phone should be taken off the hook, the television should be off, and any other distractions should be eliminated. And the time should be one that will keep distractions down as much as possible in order to be productive. Trying to solve something when you haven't eaten all day, or when you will be interrupted by children every few minutes, won't create the right climate for resolving issues. Once the setting is determined, you may begin. Just for the sake of discussion, let's walk our neighbors Frank and Sally through the issue-resolution process.

Now that the time, atmosphere, and place is right, Sally and Frank turn toward each other, and Frank, who has asked for the discussion time, should then begin to share. During this sharing time, two important stages will take place. First, the original partner should share *all* of his thoughts and his feelings. Remember the elements of the filter system that we discussed earlier? In this section, we share two of the three areas of awareness: thoughts and feelings. To tell your thoughts, describe the situation by telling what you think about what happened. And to tell your feelings, describe the emotions behind the situation.

This initial sharing time must take place *without interruption!* This means that Sally cannot verbally interrupt, but she should try to not nonverbally interrupt, either. That means no gestures, distracting body language, or deep sighs! A person can say a lot through groans or sighs, or even by feverishly taking notes while the other person is talking.

In addition, you must be careful not to use "you" or "your" statements during your sharing time. Keep it in the first person. Begin each sentence with the words "I think…," "I feel…," or "When this happened, I felt…," etc. Avoid any use of the words *you* or *your*, because "you statements" are, by default, judgmental in nature. Instead, when you use the word *I*, you are taking ownership of your thoughts, feelings, and desires.

The second stage of this step takes place when Frank has finished sharing all of his thoughts and feelings, and he is ready to turn over the discussion to his partner. At that point, the microphone, so to speak, is turned over to Sally, and she then is given the opportunity to share her thoughts and feelings about what Frank has just said to her, again using "I statements," but without interruption.

At this point, we can guarantee it will be very tempting for Frank to want to jump back in and respond to what Sally has just said: "There is one more thing you need to know," or "I don't think you really understood what I meant!" he may want to say. No matter how well-intentioned it seems, this is almost always a mistake, because 99.9 percent of the time, a response at this stage will only be bringing in another issue. It also is a setup for bantering, in which we go back and forth trying to prove our own points. This moves the discussion from gaining information to trying to influence the other person and sell them on our position. This usually only ends in further frustration and a mess on our hands. Once you have both had your time to share, that's it. The second step of the process has been completed, and it is time to move on to the third. Remember, the goal is to solve the issue, not gain a victory.

Step Three: Finding a Solution. In the solution phase, both Frank and Sally should be operating under the assumption that everything has been put on the table, and they must trust that even if misunderstandings have taken place, the solution will bring them back into focus and help them understand everything they have just discussed.

Perhaps the most important thing to remember about the solution phase is that the situation must be *behaviorally specific*. This means that Frank cannot turn to Sally and say, "I think the solution is that you should just be more considerate of me and my needs!" That is not a specific solution! It can be interpreted completely differently by both partners. Instead, Frank could say, "I want you to pick up your dirty socks and throw them into the clothes hamper." That is very behaviorally specific. In this stage, we let Frank and Sally use the words *you* and *yours* as many times as they would like. When you are seeking a solution, you are expressing what you *want,* the third part of the awareness triangle. But remember, this is not "used-car salesmanship," in which we give extreme solutions in our favor so as to get everything we want. A solution can't be one-sided, but it must be inclusive of our needs and our partner's needs. It must be something we think they may be able to agree with. It has to be win-win.

Once Frank has put his solution on the table, Sally has one of two options. She can either say, "What a brilliant solution! Let's do that from now on!" (which is unlikely or there probably wouldn't have been a conflict in the first place), or she can present an alternative solution. What she is *not* allowed to do is to say anything negative about Frank's solution. She cannot say, "Well, that is the stupidest thing I have ever heard! We're not going to do that because that *obviously* would *never* work!" Instead, she should simply say, "I can appreciate that, but my solution is…" and then present her alternative solution.

At this point, then, there are two solutions on the table, and they may be as far from each other in agreement as possible. Who wins? That's where the negotiating phase of step three comes in. After Sally has proposed her solution, the microphone goes back to Frank. He has the same two options: He can agree with Sally's solution or present yet another, taking into consideration all the solutions on the table. Solutions always need to have two things in mind: what will solve it for you *and* what will solve it for your partner. If Frank doesn't agree yet, the process is continued, alternating option after option, compromising together until one partner can say, "I agree with your solution."

At that point, there is agreement, and the power of the team has been accomplished. Two very powerful things take place when there is agreement. First, as the solution is put into place, the issue that was bothering the person who brought it up begins to go away—he or she gets rid of the negative that was coming between them. Second, when the person changes his or her behavior and agrees to do something differently to address the need, positive feelings begin to develop: *My partner does care about me and love me.* Each time new behavior takes place, the relationship begins to connect a little more, and emotional intimacy is slowly built.

What we have found in our years of counseling is that as humans, most of us really don't like to compromise! As a general rule, people are a selfish group, and most of us want our own way. But if we aren't willing to compromise on the issues that arise in our marriages (and believe us, issues *will* arise!), we will never reach the potential and reap the benefits that God has planned for our marriages.

This three-step model will take time to learn and to perfect. It is not natural and goes against the unhealthy patterns that most of us have used for years. It will take practice, so start out with some small issues and see how it can begin to change those old patterns and lead you to actually solving issues. This will allow you to put your time and energy into enjoying life together.

We are often asked, "What if my spouse does not do what he or she agreed to in the solution?" This will inevitably happen at times. What you *shouldn't* do is say, "I knew you wouldn't do what you said!" You should simply bring it up as a new issue by saying, "There is something I need to talk to you about. When would be a good time?" It really *is* a new issue—the issue now is, they didn't do what they said they would do.

Another question we hear is, "What if we can't think of another solution? Can we just say that's all I can compromise?" If you get stuck, it just means that you haven't thought of the *right* solution yet. You have to believe that there is a solution out there. You just haven't seen it yet. The best thing to do at that point is to ask for time to think and pray about it until you can come back to the table with other options. Just make sure that you *do* set a *specific* time to reconvene so that the issue doesn't get swept under the rug.

Some couples find it helpful to set a time each week for an hour to practice resolving issues so they can become skilled at this procedure and eventually be able to do it on the fly in real time. Be patient with yourself and your partner—it takes time to change old habits. But be committed to learning your new dance steps as a couple and practice new reactions to the disappointments and hurts of life.

Remember, disappointments and hurts are inevitable in life. The key is to recognize what we are feeling and stop the old "knee-jerk" reaction to those hurts and learn a new response to those feelings. As you learn this model and begin to put it into practice, you will move toward your partner, instead of away from them, in the midst of real-life challenges.

We have seen couple after couple amazed at their ability to come up with solutions that neither of them would have found on their own. Once they have tried this new way that takes the defensiveness out of the equation, they have been amazed at the creativity they have discovered. The couples realize that the blending of their views generates the best solutions and the greatest strength in their marriage. Doesn't it sound like the nature of God to have one plus one equal three?

Guess what? You're *supposed* to have issues in your marriage! To blend and mold two unique and different people together into one, issues are inevitable. It's one of the ways God chooses to mold us into the image of His Son, through the very special person He has chosen to be your mate. So issues don't mean that the relationship is over, or that you can't find a satisfactory solution. It simply means that it's time to start communicating, and begin to work on those issues that arise. When you commit to doing this in your marriage, you will begin to see God work His great design through your relationship to bless you, your children, your family, and ultimately the world, for His glory.

Team Building Exercise 8

To help you identify your marital dance steps, think back on any recent issues that you and your mate tried to deal with and identify the feelings you had when you argued. What did the interactions make you feel about yourself? Did you feel unimportant, criticized, discounted, like a failure? Write down three feelings and share them with your partner. Also, think about what you tend to do in reaction to these feelings. Do you shut down, yell, say something critical, respond sarcastically? Write down three options of what you believe you do in reaction to the feelings. Share these with your partner, and try to see how each of your reactions hit your partner's soft spot and trigger his or her own reaction. Now, remember, the point is not to try to prove who started the conflict. Both of you start the dance sometimes, but begin to act as a team and work together to see how your reactions wound your partner. The more you can be conscious of what is happening, the greater chance you each have to step out of the dance and start a new journey together.

Team Building Exercise 9

Set a time to practice the three-step, issue-resolution model. Each of you pick a very small issue and agree to use the steps as outlined in this chapter. Practice until you begin to get it, and then move to bigger issues as you have success. If you break down and can't find a solution, ask another couple whom you trust to watch you and hold you accountable to the rules until you are comfortable doing it on your own. Don't give up! The benefits are worth the effort of practicing and developing these skills in your marriage. Remember, healthy marriages are made—they are not magic.

Issue Resolution Model

I. INITIATING THE PROCESS—STAGE ONE

   A. Person 1 is aware of an issue to discuss and approaches the individual with whom he/she needs to work it out. "I have something important to talk with you about. When would be a good time?"

   B. Person 2 sets a specific time (as soon as possible, not to exceed 24 hours).

II. SHARING THE ISSUE—STAGE TWO

   A. The person who began the process introduces the issue. (Person 1). "What I want to talk about is....."

   B. Person 1 then shares his/her thoughts and feelings, without interruptions and without using the words "you" or "yours," and then Person 1 says, "I am finished."

   C. Person 2 then shares his/her thoughts and feelings, without interruption and without using the words "you" or "yours," making sure to *share about the problem presented* and not reacting to what Person 1 said about the problem; then Person 2 says, "I am finished."

III. NEGOTIATING FOR A SOLUTION—STAGE THREE

   A. Person 1, who started the first and second stages, starts this stage by offering a solution without interruption; making sure to make the solution behaviorally specific.

   B. Person 2 either accepts Person 1's solution as it is presented or he/she offers another solution in its place.

      1. Keep stage three clean; no more discussing the problem. No discussing the pros and cons of the other person's solution.

      2. Alternate sharing solutions until both persons agree with the solution.

CHAPTER 8

SEX AND ROMANCE: HOW TO KEEP THE FIRE BURNING

A successful marriage requires falling in love many times, always with the same person.
—Mignon McLaughlin

W HEN MOST PEOPLE THINK OF a happy marriage, they tend to imagine a relationship filled with passionate romance and an exciting sex life. Ironically, however, the romance and passion will be the first thing to fade if the other aspects of the relationship are not cultivated and cared for. A passionate and romantic sex life is very much a by-product of good communication, the complementing of differences, and effective issue resolution. Sexual intimacy will grow out of the emotional intimacy that is present in a healthy marriage relationship.

Unfortunately, the area of sexual intimacy is confusing for many newly married couples (as well as for those who have been married for years). Instruction in this area is not given in school or by many of our parents, and we are left to assume that it will somehow just "work itself out" when we are on the honeymoon. Despite the lack of instruction or conversation before the wedding, however, expectations in this area are certainly high—sometimes higher than in any other area. But just as in the other areas we've already addressed, men and women are wired differently, and if we don't recognize our uniqueness in this area and begin to appreciate the differences between us, one or both partners will inevitably be left unsatisfied.

Romance and the Differences between Men and Women

When we look at sexual differences, we find some significant paradoxes. Sex, for men, is a great stress-reliever, whereas women need a stress-free environment in order to feel sexual. Men use sex as a way to get close to their wives, whereas women need to feel close emotionally in order to enjoy sex. Sex is an emotional expression for men, whereas for a woman to have a fulfilling experience, sex must flow out of an intimate emotional relationship. Sounds perplexing, doesn't it? Remember, God is good, and He is not laughing at us. There is hope! A key to sexual fulfillment in marriage is for us to understand these differences and how these paradoxes can work together in harmony to build a mutually satisfying sex life with our mates.

A woman's sexual desire is directly related to how things are going in the rest of her life. If life isn't going well for her, or if things are not going smoothly in the relationship, she will generally not have a great deal of sexual desire. But if everything is going well in the relationship, and if she's happy and contented in her life overall, then her sexual desire will be a natural by-product of that satisfied life.

For most women, romance plays a key role in her life satisfaction and in the intimacy of her emotional relationship with her husband. Romance is a pervasive topic in our culture; we constantly see it demonstrated in books, movies, and television. It is generally the most popular topic of conversation around the water cooler in most offices! But the fact remains, romance is elusive to most of us—especially after we get married. The number-one complaint from women in marriage is: "Something changed. He's not like he used to be. I don't know what happened to him, but after we got married, something happened. He used to send me cards, notes, flowers, and tell me how wonderful and beautiful I was. We would stay up so late talking, and he was just incredible. But after we got married, all of that changed. At this point, I'm just lucky when he remembers my birthday!" What happened? The romance disappeared! Often the woman begins to feel that her husband doesn't love her anymore.

There is a very simple explanation for this phenomenon, and it isn't that the husband doesn't love his wife. For a man, life is task-oriented, and he is generally very focused on either accomplishing a goal or conquering an obstacle. Before the wedding, the man's focus was on "conquering" the woman by accomplishing the task of winning her over and taking her as his bride. But after that "task" was "accomplished," the man (almost always subconsciously) no longer sees the need for the cards, the compliments, the flowers—the romance. It isn't that he no longer loves her or considers her special; it's that he is wired in such a way that these things do not even cross his mind! In his mind, the next most loving task is to take care of her financially, and so he now puts this same energy into working to provide for his wife and future family.

So, by their very nature, men can miss the boat when it comes to romancing their wives. Yet if this is used as an excuse, it can create a very serious problem in their sexual relationship. Because of the natural "task focus" of a man, he can become complacent after marriage, and less active in pursuing his mate romantically and showing her how special she really is. In other words, guys, if you say, "This is just the way I am," you are shooting yourself in the foot, so to speak, because that attitude will actually dampen your wife's sexual responsiveness.

Your wives *need* romance in order to connect with you! And that "romance" may not be exactly what you think it is. For a woman, romance is more than just receiving flowers or a card; it is the amount of effort and thoughtfulness that went into the gesture. Suppose that a husband presents his wife with a bouquet of flowers one evening, and when she asked what the occasion was, he answered, "Well, the secretary at work got flowers, but she was on her way out of town so she told me to bring them home to you. And you say I never bring you flowers!" How would she react? She certainly wouldn't feel very loved or appreciated! So it's not the flowers *themselves* that create the romance; it's the thought behind the flowers that is important.

When a woman receives a thoughtful gesture from her husband, she feels loved and cared for. She thinks, *We are still boyfriend and girlfriend!* It breeds excitement, love, and passion in her heart, and it causes her to feel connected with her mate in a way that nothing else can. Not only that, but it increases her self-esteem, and as we have seen, a woman draws the majority of her self-esteem from her primary love relationships. If she is feeling courted and loved, and her self-esteem begins to grow in the relationship, it is only natural that her sexual desire will begin to grow.

I (Brent) know it seems that a major focus in this chapter is men beginning to understand the needs of their wives. That is on purpose—because men are to be the leaders. Men have often misunderstood leadership, believing it is all about being "large and in charge" and making all the final decisions. I believe we have missed the point. Leadership means that men are to love their wives as "Christ loved the church." He literally gave His life for the church. Jesus was the ultimate servant-leader. Leadership means that men should live their lives in such a way that others want to follow them. They should be the first to sacrifice their needs for others, the first to give, the first to say "I am sorry," the ones who make sure they are communicating well, resolving issues with win/win solutions, etc. If men do their part, their wives will respond in marvelous ways. If men are selfish and ego-driven, their wives have nothing positive to respond to.

Therefore, in sexuality, men need to begin to *purposefully* cultivate romance in their relationships with their wives. Because men are made by God to be givers, and women were created to be receivers, it is important to make the decision to honor our wives in the same way that Christ loved His Church. When we begin to learn *romance* as a *task* that we can perform that will show our wives their significance and value, the intimacy and passion in the marriage will grow, and soon a more intimate and satisfying sex life will be the result.

Sexual Desire and the Differences between Men and Women

When a woman begins to be "wooed" again by her husband, sex will become infinitely more enjoyable and passionate for her. Part of this is due to the difference between the sexual responses of men and women.

Men. For most men, the only prerequisite for an interest in having sex is whether or not they have a pulse and are breathing! A man can have a terrible day at work, even get fired from his job, get a speeding ticket on the way home, run over his kid's tricycle in the driveway, get out and break his toe on the door-jamb on the way inside the house, and still be ready to have sex at a moment's notice. He is wired to be ready "in season and out," primarily because for a man, sex is an "action statement," a means to an end.

For men, sex demonstrates affection. When he is making love, it is a powerful time of connection for him, allowing him to draw close to his wife, demonstrate loving feelings to her (without necessarily needing to talk or use words!), and experience a powerful physical release.

Women. For women, just about the opposite is true. If a woman had the same kind of day that the man had—getting fired, getting a speeding ticket, and wrecking the car—and then if later that night, she were tapped on the shoulder by her husband and asked, "Are you interested?" chances are, she'd respond, "In what?" And if he were to actually explain, she'd likely say, "Are you crazy??"

For a woman, if things are not going well in her life, sex is probably not even an option. It may not even cross her mind. Sexual desire is something that grows out of a satisfied life, and if life is not going well, and especially if there is an unresolved conflict in the relationship, sex may be the absolute last thing in the world she will be interested in.

We have some dear friends who tell the story of one night when he rolled over in bed and snuggled up to her. She immediately recognized his intentions and said, "Honey, the kids are sick!" He immediately replied, "Sweetheart, the *kids* are sick, not *you!*"

That statement just shows that when something is out of sync in a woman's life, she's not likely to respond positively to the "overtures of love" being sent to her by her husband! On the other hand, however, women do need to recognize that they go through a certain decision-making process when they are approached for sex. Wives tend to get irritated that their husbands may need to "make a decision" to be romantic. They wonder: *Why doesn't it come from him naturally? Why does he have to* decide *to be romantic with me?* But when it comes to sex, women do something very similar. When a husband begins to snuggle up or caress, almost immediately the majority of wives begin to go through a list in their minds: *Okay, obviously he wants to have sex. Let's see, it's 11 o'clock now, and I have to get up at 6:30. I've still got to fold the laundry yet tonight, but that won't be done for another 30 minutes. I'm sort of tired, but it would be better to do this now than later, especially since I've got to get up so early.*

Women honestly make a decision about whether or not they are willing to have sex! Where romance is not as natural for a man, and he has to make a decision to be romantic with his wife, women are the same way sexually—they make a decision about being sexually intimate with their husbands.

Much of the issue boils down to respecting these differences. If we respect the fact that we are "wired" differently, and begin to work to bridge these differences, it is amazing what a satisfying intimate relationship can be experienced in marriage.

Top 21 Sexual Myths

Even with this understanding in place, however, there are several myths regarding sexuality that are pervasive in our culture. These must be addressed in order for a satisfying sexual marriage relationship to take place. The following list of our "Top 21 Sexual Myths" are *not* true, so if you find yourself agreeing with one or more of them, it may be hindering your sex life. Sex is a gift from God, but it has been treated with little respect by our culture, which has prevented many people from experiencing God's best.

1. Lovemaking must always involve sex. Sometimes just cuddling and caressing are enough for pleasurable sexual intimacy, particularly for women. This goes along with myth number 2:

2. Pleasurable physical contact must always lead to sex. A woman needs what is considered to be eight to twelve "meaningful touches" each day to feel connected and close to her partner, and for a woman, most meaningful touches do *not* involve sex.[1] Many women are frustrated by this because when many men touch, they are doing so for sexual purposes. Husbands need to learn how to touch and caress their wives in ways that are meaningful *to them,* and that do not necessarily lead to the act of sex itself. A basic need for a woman is non-sexual touch and non-sexual closeness, and the more a man can fulfill this need, the more likely a woman is to be receptive to sexual intimacy.

One of the greatest things a man can do to show his wife that he loves and cares for her is a principle called "pleasuring,"[2] the giving and receiving of non-sexual pleasure. This is something of a sacrifice for a man, because it involves touching and caressing his wife, without sex being the object in mind. But it makes a profound statement to her that says, "I want to be close and I want to nurture you, and I'm not looking for anything in return."

3. You can't participate in lovemaking and enjoy it unless you feel sexual. There are times when you can make a decision to have sex, even if you don't feel particularly sexual at that moment. However, if a woman does this too many times, sex may begin to feel more like an obligation to her, and nothing will kill her sexual desire faster than that feeling. She needs to have the right to say "no" without any repercussions, or her sexual desire may eventually begin to die. Men, if you give your wife the freedom to say "no," she will likely say "yes" more often in the long run.

4. Sex must always lead to orgasm. A woman can experience pleasure in sex without having an orgasm, but that is something that men have a very difficult time understanding. That is where good communication can make a difference. If a woman feels respected and that she has the choice to say "yes," she can choose to be sexual with her husband even if it is not the perfect time—just to bless him and meet his emotional and physical needs. In other words, it can still be a positive experience for her. However, men, this does not negate the need to nourish your wife, focusing on *her* emotional and sexual needs.

5. Once started, sex must always continue until orgasm has been achieved. For a woman, operating under this myth can put an enormous amount of pressure on the sex act. Sometimes achieving orgasm takes more time and energy than the woman can invest at that time. A woman can still enjoy sex without an orgasm, even though that would not be the same for her husband. Sex without orgasm is okay for the women as long as it is a choice she makes at the time and that her full satisfaction is fulfilled at other times.

6. A couple should reach orgasm at the same time. Again, this myth puts too much pressure on the experience, and each person tends to be focusing so much on the timing that they forget to just relax and enjoy it. But when you realize that this may not always happen at the same time—and that's okay—it can alleviate a lot of sexual stress.

7. Sex must be spontaneous to really be good. Most of us have very busy and scheduled lives in which it is hard to find time to be sexually intimate with our spouses. In the movies and on television, however, we always see these wild escapades at the office or all over different parts of the house. Don't you ever wonder where everyone else is when these antics are taking place? Where is the guy in the next cubicle over, or the neighbors or kids or even pets? The fact is, there are times when if sex weren't planned, it might not happen at all! If I plan a vacation, that doesn't mean that the vacation isn't as good because I didn't just hop on a plane and go. Many times the vacation is better because of the anticipation and excitement that goes into planning the event!

8. It's performance that really counts. Sex should be fun! Don't get so caught up in your performance or that of your partner that you feel too much pressure to enjoy it!

9. Sexual ability comes naturally. You can learn to be a good lover! But the best way to learn how to really please your partner is to talk to him or her. Communication is key to a great sex life.

10. Good sex must be "super sex." Everything else in our lives has "good days" and "bad days"—why do we think that sex should be any different? Sex is just like anything else—sometimes it's incredible and sometimes it's just okay. We are going to have different experiences at different times, and that's okay.

11. Men should be active during sex, and women should be passive. This goes along with myth number 12:

12. In sex, as in dancing, men must take the lead and women must follow. These are antiquated ideas that we've heard for years, but they just aren't true. You need to discover the relationship that's the most satisfying for you. How do you do that? Overcome myth 13:

13. It's not okay to try anything new. With good communication in place, it's always a good idea to break out of the routine and discover something new and exciting in the bedroom—or living room, dining room, or backyard! Your partner will not know what you want to try if you don't tell them. Don't force your partner to mind read what brings you pleasure, but also, when trying something new, don't allow them to do things that make you uncomfortable without sharing your feelings.

14. You're either good or bad at sex. Again, you can learn—especially when you have good, open communication with your partner and a sense of adventure!

15. It's a good idea to have sex before marriage to determine if we are sexually compatible. The truth is actually just the opposite. One of the greatest complications to a sex life after marriage is when premarital sex has taken place.

16. The honeymoon is the sexual peak of marriage; it's "all downhill" from there. The truth is also just the opposite. The honeymoon might actually be your most awkward time sexually as a couple. From there, you begin to learn how to please each other, you learn more about each other's bodies, and you learn new techniques. The best is yet to come!

17. Your appearance dictates your sexual performance. Nothing could be farther from the truth.

18. Having had multiple partners makes you a better lover. Actually, having had multiple partners causes more complications.

19. Once sex has turned bad in a marriage, there's not much hope. Anything can be improved—especially the sexual aspect of a marriage. God is in the restoration business, and there is always hope.

20. Sexual desire can't be increased. This is absolutely false. There are many, many things you can do to increase your own sexual desire and that of your spouse, starting with beginning to inject the passion and romance back into the relationship! Because sex is a natural by-product of all of the other aspects of the relationship, any improvement in any other area can bring improvement in your sex life.

And now for the final myth:

21. In this enlightened age, none of these myths has had any influence on my marriage. This is the greatest myth of all! If, however, you begin to recognize which myths have played a role in your life, and which may have even brought harm to your marriage, you can begin to make the necessary corrections and see a whole new revitalization in your love life!

A Practical Suggestion for Romance: Date Night

Obviously romance is important for a healthy sex life, along with correct information and an understanding of the differences between a husband and wife. Earlier in this book, we discussed the concept of the Love Bank, in which both people invest into and make withdrawals from the relationship and each other. Each time a loving act is performed—a word, a gesture, a meaningful touch, a specific action—deposits are made. What often happens, however, is that more withdrawals are made than deposits, especially due to the busyness of our lives, and soon the emotion and the spark in the marriage begins to die.

Happy marriages are ones that have good healthy habits in place. In all of our years of working with couples, one of the most powerful weekly habits that we have seen do wonders for couples is a weekly "Date Night," a night scheduled and set aside for the two of you to reconnect and rekindle the passion of your relationship.

Here are our practical suggestions for Date Night.

1. Choose fun and enjoyable activities only! This is not the time to work on a budget or try to deal with some other conflict between you. Everything else needs to be set aside in order to simply have fun together. We are conditioned creatures. If you get into any heavy issues on your date, it won't be remembered as a pleasant event. You will think about that the next time a date is planned and will tend to shy away from these times— even if only subconsciously. Keep it fun, even if you have to work at it to get it started.

2. Date Night is for the two of you only. This isn't "family time" with the kids, nor is it a night to double date with another couple. It's reconnection time for the two of you, and you alone.

3. Date Night should be a top priority every week. There will always seem to be something more important to do, but unless you make it a top priority, it just won't happen. Determine to choose your marriage as a top priority.

4. Try to have your Date Night take place at the same time every week, if at all possible. This is especially helpful for babysitting or other schedules and, quite frankly, to keep it from being forgotten.

5. Date Night should be planned. So many times, couples will get in the car, look at each other, and the questions will begin: "What do you want to do?" "I don't know—what do you want to do?" But, husbands, when you first asked your wife out on a date, was that what you did? No, you washed the car, you planned out the activities, you made reservations, you took cash out of the bank—you were prepared! What that said to your sweetheart was, "You are valuable. I've been thinking about you all day." The same thing should happen on Date Night!

It needs to be planned, but the key to making this work in the long run is that it be fair. It's not fair to have one person do the planning all of the time. So we recommend the planning and preparation for the date be alternated between partners every week. Which leads to suggestion number 6:

6. Make a Top Ten list of Date Nights. Write out in detail what your favorite Date Nights would be, and then exchange the papers. When it is your week to decide, choose from the options on your partner's list. This gives you the opportunity to plan for and surprise your partner with something they really want to do. It can be really fun to try to "out-give" each other with ideas!

7. Be as creative as possible. Don't be afraid to try something new!

8. Pick a financial limit. Many couples shy away from Date Night because they think it will take a lot of money that they don't have. But Date Night can fit into any couple's budget. Think back to the time when you were dating. Remember how it didn't really matter what you did, as long as you were together? Walks in the park, window shopping, browsing in a bookstore—all of these are free! You can make Date Night as expensive or inexpensive as you want it to be.

Along with that, we understand that babysitting costs can get expensive when you are going out every week. We often encourage couples to get together and do a babysitting exchange. One couple watches both sets of kids one night, and the next night the other couple reciprocates. That way, both couples get their Date Night, and the kids can become friends too!

Consistent date nights create intimacy. They help you to reconnect each week, and they will have a positive effect on every part of your marriage. They are definitely worth the time and effort!

Remember, feelings follow behaviors. You can choose the level of warmth and passion in your marriage because you can choose your behavior. If you choose well, you can keep the romance and passion alive in your marriage. When you do so, the satisfaction you gain will be so much more than you ever expected—and the benefits will be lifelong. Remember, great marriages are not the result of magic; great marriages are made through the decisions that you make on a daily basis. Choose to have the passionate partnership that God intended for you to have.

Team Building Exercise 10

Talk about starting a Date Night.

- Pick a night.
- Make your list of ideas.
- Decide who will choose the first activity.
- Decide on the budget.
- Commit to getting started.

Team Building Exercise 11

Set a time to go over the sexual-myths list with each other and discuss your impressions.

CONCLUSION

MARRIAGE IS A MARVELOUS PLAN that God designed for our benefit. Our challenge is that as humans we have a limited understanding of the ways of God, and therefore we struggle with this most sacred and powerful relationship. As we have seen throughout the pages of this book, marriage is only effective if we are able to give outwardly from our life to another and love another as we have been loved by God, who is never self-centered but is always focused on giving from His life to our lives.

We have two final thoughts to share with you as we come to the close of this writing. First, all of the intentions of our hearts are of no avail if we do not implement the behavior that comes out of our hearts' desire to love our partners. Over the last few chapters of this book, we have looked at what the behavior of love looks like in a marriage and the fact that the *feelings* of love are a by-product of the *behaviors* of love. We have ended each chapter with exercises that can help you put these loving behaviors in play in your marriages. As we close, it is important to recognize that each of us has a choice. We can hear these ideas and think good thoughts about them and what they could do to bring life to our marriages—and do nothing—and they will end up being merely good ideas with no effect on our lives. Or we can begin to practice these behaviors and give our marriages an infusion of life. Which behavior stood out to you most as the one you believe that your marriage needs? That would be a good place to start. You may be able to think of several—if that is the case, pick the easiest one just to get the ball rolling.

Don't close the last page of this book without asking God to help you begin to make your marriage more into the image He designed it to be. He has a *good* future planned for you, but you are the one who holds the key and must make the first move.

Second, we want you to remember that our ability to love our mates as God loves us depends a great deal on our ability to gain strength from God to do so. The reason that some relationships don't flourish is that instead of marriage being a love relationship flowing out of the overflow of God's provision and love in our own hearts, we are trying to get our core human needs for love and significance met through our spouse. No human was ever intended to be God in our lives. No other human will ever be able to love us in a way that nourishes the deepest recesses of our hearts. That is why so many people are left longing for more in their marriages—their focus is on the wrong source. If I am dependent on my sense of personal value being given to me by another person, I will remain thirsty, because they were not designed to fill that need in my life. Healthy marriages are the overflow of the loving life of two individuals who are filled with the love of God and who allow that love to overflow toward each other.

Therefore, we can work hard to put all of the practices in this book into place, but if we are attempting to do so in our own strength, our efforts will ultimately fall short. Our will must be daily turned over to the will of God for His love and strength, so that He may be the source of the love in our hearts toward our spouse. God wants to be this Source for your life, and His love for you is far more significant than you will ever be able to imagine.

You have great worth apart from your performance because Christ gave His life for you and therefore imparted great value to you. You are deeply loved, fully pleasing, totally forgiven, accepted, and complete in Christ![1]

> *Who shall separate us from the love of Christ? Shall trouble or hardship or persecution or famine or nakedness or danger or sword? ... No, in all these things we are more than conquerors through him who loved us. For I am convinced that neither death nor life, neither angels nor demons, neither the present nor the future, nor any powers, neither height nor depth, nor anything else in all creation, will be able to separate us from the love of God that is in Christ Jesus our Lord.*
>
> —Romans 8:35–39

ENDNOTES

Chapter 1

[1] Helen Fisher, *The Anatomy of Love* (W.W. Norton & Company, 1992).

[2] Ibid.

Chapter 2

[1] John M. Gottman, *The Marriage Clinic* (W.W. Norton & Company, 1999).

[2] Willard J. Harley, *His Needs, Her Needs* (Grand Rapids, Mich.: Baker, 2001).

[3] Gary Chapman, *The Five Love Languages* (Chicago: Moody, 2004).

[4] Tim LaHaye, *Spirit-Controlled Temperament,* Revised Ed. (Wheaton, Tyndale House Publishers, Inc. 1992)

Chapter 3

[1] Gary Smalley, *Hidden Keys to Loving Relationships,* (Relationships Today, 1988)

[2] Ibid

[3] Ibid

[4] Ibid

[5] Ibid

[6] Ibid

[7] Anne Moir & David Jessel, *Brain Sex* (New York, Dell Publishing, 1992)

[8] Ibid

[9] Dr. Donald Joy, *Innate Differences Between Men and Women* (Focus on the Family, 1993)

[10] Ibid

[11] Ibid

Chapter 4

[1] Tim LaHaye, *Spirit-Controlled Temperament*, (Wheaton, Il. Tyndale House Publishers, 1984)

[2] Florence Littauer, *Personality Plus* (Grand Rapids, Mich.: Baker, 1992).

Chapter 5

[1] Lewis B. Smedes, *Forgive and Forget: Healing the Hurts We Don't Deserve* (San Francisco: HarperSanFrancisco, 1984), xvii-xix.

Chapter 6

[1] MaeLynn K. Harris, "Brains Get In the Way of Words When Men and Women Talk," Hard News Café, January 17, 2002, http://www.hardnewscafe.usu.edu/features/index.html

[2] Cathy Cartoon

[3] Gary Smalley, *Hidden Keys to Loving Relationships*, (Relationships Today, 1988)

[4] Dr. Donald Joy, *Innate Differences Between Men and Women* (Focus on the Family, 1993)

[5] Ibid

[6] Ibid

[7] See note 3 above.

Chapter 7

[1] John M. Gottman, *The Marriage Clinic* (W.W. Norton & Company, 1999).

[2] Kevin Leman, *The Pleasers* (New York, New York, Dell Publishing, 1987)

Chapter 8

[1] Gary Smalley, *Hidden Keys to Loving Relationships*, (Relationships Today, 1988)

[2] Dr. Ed and Gaye Wheat, *Intended for Pleasure*, Third Edition, Rev. Ed. (Grand Rapids, Mi. Fleming H. Revell, 1997)

Conclusion

[1] Robert McGee, *The Search for Significence*, Rev. ed. (Nashville, Tn., W Publishing Group, 2003.)

ABOUT THE
AUTHORS

May 1, 1978

December 1, 2005

Brent and Janis Sharpe are licensed marriage and family counselors, and since 1982, they have helped thousands of couples maximize and heal their marriages and relationships. They are founders of The Life Connection Counseling Center in Tulsa, OK, and Brent is Co-Senior Pastor of the Life Connection Church in Jenks, Oklahoma. Brent and Janis were married in 1978 and are the proud parents of four children, Preston, Kaitlin, Spencer, and Hayley.

Brent is a Licensed Professional Counselor and Brent and Janis both are Licensed Marriage and Family Therapists. Brent and Janis travel the country sharing their experiences through marriage seminars and training leadership in premarital, marriage, and family counseling.

CONTACT
INFORMATION

AS PART OF THEIR MINISTRY and counseling outreach, Brent and Janis conduct marriage and parenting seminars and relationship building workshops for churches and ministries. They have also developed an extensive premarital counselor training program designed to help pastors and churches develop a mentor couple premarital counseling program.

To contact Brent and Janis to conduct a marriage seminar, speaking engagement, or for more information on the lay counselor program, please contact them via their Web site at:

www.brentandjanissharpe.com

Or by mail:

The Life Connection Counseling Center
7145 S. Braden St.
Tulsa, OK 74136

PREMARITAL COUNSELING

HAVING A GOOD PREMARITAL COUNSELING program is the best way for churches to insure healthy marriages. Brent and Janis have developed a complete 12-week course for churches to use in counseling couples.

Courses include:
- Step-by-step leaders training manual
- Training sessions on DVD and CD
- Testing materials
- Detailed couples' workbook
- Interactive exercises and diagrams

Topics include:
- Managing expectations
- Understanding three major areas of differences: Gender, Personality, Environment
- Communication and issue resolution
- Roles and responsibilities
- Managing money
- Sex and romance
- Spiritual development

For more information on purchasing the marital counseling program or other counseling books and materials, please go to the Web site:

www.brentandjanissharpe.com

are you a
HERO
or just a
HUSBAND?

- ✓ Never again forget an important date.
- ✓ Receive ongoing encouragement and reminders to effectively communicate love to your wife & children.
- ✓ Experience scriptural insight to empower you in your personal life.

*For just **$4.95 a month** you can obtain **"hero status."***

30-Day
Sign up today for a FREE TRIAL

mensreminders!.com